I Love You, Holy Spirit

I Love You, Holy Spirit
A Journey of Adventure, Outpouring, and Miracles

This book is set in the typeface *Athelas* designed by Veronika Burian and Jose Scaglione.

Paperback ISBN: 978-1-967262-46-5
Hardcover ISBN: 979-8-2955-7583-9

A Publication of *Tall Pine Books*
PO Box 42 Warsaw | Indiana 46581
www.tallpinebooks.com

| 1 26 26 20 16 02 |

Published in the United States of America

I Love You, Holy Spirit

A Journey of Adventure, Outpouring, and Miracles

ANTHONY RAY CASTRO

Endorsements

Anthony Castro is like a supernatural James Bond—an international man of adventure... with the Holy Spirit.

It is easy—and truly a joy—to endorse a book from someone you trust, from someone whose writings are absolutely congruent with his lifestyle. Anthony is a true practitioner of revival, and it is with genuine delight that I recommend him, his ministry, and this book to you. Perhaps most notably in this case, his words (which you are now reading in manuscript form) have literally caused my heart to burn for more of Jesus.

While ministering with Anthony in Tasmania, I vividly remember driving around together, enjoying the sights, laughing uproariously, and delighting in some fine cuisine. But everything shifted when he began to talk about what he has so brilliantly and vividly described in the pages set before you: how he met the Holy Spirit, the Kathryn Kuhlman meeting that changed everything, and what it looks like to enjoy a life of true adventure with the Spirit of God.

When sharing about these testimonies, his words brought us right into those encounters with God and the Spirit's holy presence filled the car.

This is not someone offering rigid formulas on how to "pursue a relationship with the Holy Spirit like me," where we feel we must do exactly what the author did in order to secure the same holy results. Nope. Let this book wash over you, reader. It's not a list of "how-tos," but a stunning glimpse of what's possible for the one who fully surrenders his or her life to the Holy Spirit.

It will look different from person to person—and it should—because of how uniquely God has made each one of us. One thing is certain, though: it's meant to be an adventure, a lifestyle of ongoing discovery and encounter with the Glorious One we call the Holy Spirit.

LARRY SPARKS, MDIV.
Sparks Ministries
Bestselling Author of *Pentecostal Fire*
VP of Publishing, *Destiny Image*

I have had the privilege of ministering and staying with Anthony and his beautiful family. He is the real deal who carries the heart of a revivalist, and I can honestly say this book carries the same thing he carries in real life, a genuine, tender love for the Holy Spirit that's not about hype or image. *I Love You, Holy Spirit* isn't written to impress you, it's written to invite you. It reads like someone opening up their journal and saying, "Come closer… there's more."

What I appreciate most is how personal it is. It doesn't feel like a "how-to" manual, it feels like a doorway into a relationship, the kind that shifts your everyday life, not just your church moments. If you're hungry for the presence of God, if you've been asking for more, or if you just want to fall in love with the Holy Spirit again in a real way, this book will stir you.

I'm grateful Anthony put this on paper. It's honest, full of faith, and it will make you want to slow down, listen, and draw near. I highly recommend it not just because he's my friend, but because what's in these pages is the real thing. I would encourage anyone to get a copy and go on a journey of discovering just how much Holy Spirit wants to invade your life.

JOSHUA SAWIRIS
Senior leader, *Glory City Nashville*
www.glorycitynashville.com

I Love You, Holy Spirit is a deeply moving invitation into an intimate relationship with the Holy Spirit. In this book Anthony Ray Castro shares encounters that stir faith, awaken hunger, and point unmistakably to the undeniable power of the Holy Spirit. These pages carry the fragrance of a life walked closely with God. Through Anthony's compelling experiences, readers will be reminded that the Holy Spirit is not a doctrine to study, but a Person to know; near, personal, and still powerfully at work today. Holy Spirit, I love you!

ANDRES BISONNI
Christian Evangelist, Conference Speaker
& Author of *My Beloved Holy Spirit*
www.HolySpirit.tv

Anthony Castro writes not from theory, but from a life deeply acquainted with the Person of the Holy Spirit. These pages carry a sacred invitation—away from religion and into intimate, daily fellowship with God's abiding presence. This book will stir hunger, awaken wonder, and gently lead readers into a living relationship with the Holy Spirit who is near, personal, and powerfully real. It is not merely a testimony—it is an open door into a holy adventure.

TOMMY & MIRIAM EVANS
Revival Mandate International
Best selling authors of *Decrees that Activate the Gifts of The Holy Spirit*
www.revivalmandate.org

Dedication

Some moments mark you forever.

As a young boy—and again as a teenager—I found myself sitting in meetings led by Kathryn Kuhlman, unaware that God was quietly shaping the course of my life. At the time, I lacked the language to describe what I was encountering, yet I was meeting the Person of the Holy Spirit in a way I had never known before.

There was a freedom in those services. A holy weight. A tenderness and power that reached far beyond anything I had experienced in church life up to that point.

The presence of God was so tangible that it reshaped my understanding of who He is—how great He is—and what life with Him could truly look like. I watched with my own eyes as people were healed—sick, lame, and broken—without any natural explanation. It was not a spectacle. It was love. It was the miracle-working power of the Holy Spirit revealing the deep compassion of Jesus for humanity.

Those moments did far more than inspire me; they altered the trajectory of my faith, my ministry, and my understanding of God's glory. They awakened a lifelong hunger to know the Holy Spirit not merely as a doctrine, but as a living, present Person—faithful, gentle, and powerful.

I am forever indebted to Ms. Kuhlman for her journey of faith, her sacrifice, and her unwavering devotion to making Jesus known. She never sought a platform for herself; she consistently pointed people to Him. She lived with a profound reverence for the Holy Spirit and paid a personal price to walk in obedience, purity, and surrender. Because of that, generations—myself included—have been deeply touched.

This book is dedicated to a pioneer of faith: a woman who paved the way for millions to encounter Jesus and to know His precious Holy Spirit more deeply and intimately.

Thank you, Kathryn Kuhlman. Thanks a million for saying yes.

With deep gratitude,
ANTHONY RAY CASTRO

Contents

Foreword

I remember many years ago discovering an incredible woman's life and ministry by the name of Kathryn Kuhlman. As I studied her life and listened to her teachings, read books about her and the glorious testimonies that flowed from her meetings, I was undone by her intimacy with the Holy Spirit. The purity and awe of God she lived in and her deep, unapologetic, unrestrained communion with the Holy Spirit ignited hunger so deep in me to know Him more deeply. I remember hearing the words quoted that she spoke:

"He is more real to me than any person seated here."

Her close proximity and nearness to the Holy Spirit, the way she walked in the most beautiful divine dance with Him, loving Him, beholding Him in His beauty with every breath, oh how the fragrance of her intimacy with the Holy Spirit fell upon me time and time again as I read and listened and watched, as fire, fuelling the deep cry and groan of faith within me "Nothing is impossible for those who believe" and to be one who walked like Kathryn Kuhlman in deep reverence, obedience and a life deeply surrendered and yielded to Him, His ways and His Word. The way I watched heaven respond to her yes and her faith, which saw His power manifest through a laid down life to touch, transform and heal countless people for the Glory of God.

Watching her life lived out, seeing the beautiful heart and life of Christ manifested again and again and again through miracle working power, because of her nearness to Him marked my life. I was deeply transformed, impacted and changed by the move of the Holy Spirit through Kathryn Kuhlman, undone by the daily invitation into deeper and deeper communion with the Holy Spirit and the goodness of God spread across the earth through His miracle working power. Such deep hunger was ignited within me, deeper than I had ever known.

As I read this incredible book by my dear friend Anthony Castro, that deep hunger and fire within me for deeper and deeper communion with the Holy Spirit blazed even stronger. Reading part of Anthony's journey and the glorious testimonies contained within this book calls you higher, it calls you deeper, the invitation is extended again to deeper and deeper communion with the Holy Spirit. Anthony is one who lives with such a deep laid down surrender and yes to the Lord, the purity that he carries and walks in and the faith that he walks in to take the Lord at His Word and to move with Him, has deeply blessed me over many, many years of friendship.

Anthony writes in this incredible book:

"I learned that true fruitfulness flows from fellowship, and that spiritual power is not sustained by striving, but by presence."

These very words are words that I have watched Anthony live by, one who longs for and dwells in His presence and he lives a life of true fruitfulness revealing the nature of Christ and His powerful works in the earth.

As I read one of Anthony's moments with Jesus where Jesus spoke to him opening up a deeper invitation that redirected the course of his life:

"Anthony, learn to know My Spirit. Spend time with Him. Love Him - He loves you. Learn to listen and to hear His voice."

Intimacy. Anthony is a true friend of God and this book is not only a gift to you and to the body of Christ, but this book is a well of transformation, encounter and invitation to come deeper into communion with the Holy Spirit.

As you approach this book with hunger and surrender, I guarantee you as you read these pages, revival fire will mark you afresh. You will be transformed by the testimonies of incredible wonder working power of our beautiful Jesus, and the invitation to come up higher into following the Lord's leading and His ways, whatever that looks like, will encourage and challenge you as you read Anthony's story. This book carries such a weighty impartation of faith, I know as you read these pages postured before the Lord for all He has for you within these pages, your faith will be ignited to see the impossible made possible in greater ways.

As I closed the final page of this book, the cry in my heart was louder than it has ever been...

"I love you Holy Spirit."

"I want to know You even more deeply."

I was gripped by the heart of God for deeper intimacy with me and partnering with Him to see the wonder working power of Jesus released through my life and I know you will experience and encounter the same passion on the heart of God for you as you read these pages.

Thank you, Anthony for penning such an incredible, anointed, rich book, a gift from the Lord's heart for the Church and the world, thank you for capturing the heart of God for communion with the Holy Spirit in such a beautiful way, for such a time as this.

All for His Glory!

LANA VAWSER
Prophetic Voice and Author of *The Prophetic Voice of God, A Time to Selah, I hear the Lord say New Era,* and *Woman of God, Fully Alive*

Introduction

There are words we say about God, and then there are words we learn to say *to* Him. And then there are the words we whisper when we finally realize how near He has been all along.

* * *

I awoke early, before the sun had fully risen. For a moment, I lay still—aware, even before I opened my eyes, that something was different.

My room was not empty.

It was filled—saturated, even—with the Shekinah glory of God. The atmosphere itself felt alive, heavy yet gentle, unmistakably marked by His presence. I hadn't been seeking an experience. I hadn't planned this moment. Yet there it was—holy, quiet, and undeniable.

I recognized Him.

My heart began to race as questions stirred within me. How could this be? Had the same glory I encountered the night before in a Kathryn Kuhlman miracle service followed me home? Had that rapturous moment in Kansas City truly ended—or was this only the beginning?

Then, from deep within me—unplanned and unforced—words rose effortlessly to my lips. With awe and quiet joy, I whispered the greeting that welled up from my spirit:

"Good morning, Holy Spirit!"

How could I not greet Him? How could I remain silent when the very One who had been introduced to me the night before—the One who had revealed Himself so tangibly through Mrs. Kuhlman's ministry—was now resting in and over my room, filling it with His presence?

That morning became a holy landmark for me. A threshold. A beginning. Not of religion—but of relationship. I didn't understand everything then, and I didn't yet have language for what was happening. But I knew this much: I had been invited into a journey—a daily walk of fellowship with the Spirit of God.

He was not distant; He was my Helper. My Comforter. My Strengthener. The One who would always lead me to Jesus and stand by me through every trial, just as He stood beside Jesus during His earthly ministry.

Over the years, I would come to know many things

about His ways—His whispers and His power, His tenderness and His guidance. But that morning remains the beginning for me. It was the day the veil lifted, and I discovered that the Holy Spirit was not merely an influence or a force; He is a Person. A Friend. The precious gift the Father has given to us through the Son.

This book was not written as a theology of the Holy Spirit, nor as a manual on spiritual experiences. It was born out of relationship—one that unfolded slowly, tenderly, and sometimes unexpectedly. It is the story of how God introduced me, again and again, to His nearness and His power through the Person of the Holy Spirit.

For many years, I loved God deeply. I knew the Father's heart. I treasured the grace of my Savior, Jesus Christ. Yet if I am honest, the Holy Spirit remained, for a long time, at the edges of my understanding—present, powerful, but not yet personal. I knew about Him long before I truly knew Him.

That began to change as I learned a simple, life-altering truth: God has not left us alone, nor did He ever intend for us to walk our journey in Christ here on earth alone. Instead, He has given us the Beloved Person of the Holy Spirit—what greater gift could the Father give to His Son's Bride than His own abiding presence?

Just as Christ lovingly gave Himself to cleanse and prepare a people for Himself, the Holy Spirit now works within us to make us ready. The Holy Spirit has come to glorify Christ, revealing His life and power to us and gently beautifying the Bride. He is drawing us into intimacy, forming Christ within us, and preparing us for the coming day of union and joy. It is the Lord's desire that we come to know Him, become intimately acquainted with Him, and love, worship, and honour Him as we do the Father and the Son.

The Holy Spirit is not an abstract force, a distant influence, or a theological concept reserved for a select few. He is God Himself—present, gentle, powerful, and deeply personal. He reveals Jesus, carries the heart of the Father, and walks with us through both ordinary days and impossible moments.

The Invitation

As the years unfolded, I became more intimately acquainted with Him and began to cherish my times of fellowship so deeply that ministry gradually moved to second place, while intimate relationship came first. I learned that true fruitfulness flows from fellowship, and that spiritual power is not sustained by striving, but by presence.

In one such sacred moment, Jesus Himself spoke to me—not with instruction, but with invitation. His words, quiet yet weighty, gently redirected the course of my life:

"Anthony, learn to know My Spirit.
Spend time with Him.
Love Him—He loves you.
Learn to listen and to hear His voice."

What He offered was not performance, but intimacy.

The miracles witnessed in Kathryn Kuhlman's ministry were neither coincidence nor accident. They flowed from a deep, reverent relationship with the Holy Spirit. She understood what few grasped so clearly—that the Holy Spirit is not merely a power to be used, but a Person to be revered and loved. He is the One who manifests the life of Christ, releases the miracle-working power of Jesus, and glorifies the Son in the earth.

By cultivating intimacy, fellowship, and obedience to the Holy Spirit, Kathryn saw Heaven touch earth, and through her obedience, multitudes were touched. Through that same kind of relationship, I began to see the life of Christ revealed again and again—not because of gifting or position, but because of nearness. The miracles that astonished believers, skeptics, and even atheists were expressions of God's mercy and grace, extended to the just and the unjust through the loving ministry of the Holy Spirit.

This book is a collection of those encounters.

Some are dramatic.

Many are quiet.

All of them carry the same truth:

When we simply yield our lives to God—just as we are—He meets us there. As Kathryn Kuhlman often said, "God is not looking for golden vessels or silver vessels. He is looking for yielded vessels." It is in surrender, not perfection, that God finds room to move. When a heart is yielded, Heaven responds, and God pours His life, power, and grace through those who are willing to say yes.

Within these pages, you will journey across nations and into hidden places—classrooms concealed from the world, hospital rooms saturated with prayer, and midnight moments when Heaven presses in close. You will encounter stories from the Middle East and beyond—moments where the Holy Spirit reveals Himself in breathtaking ways: His power released, His faithfulness displayed, His nearness felt, and His living reality unmistakably known.

This is not a distant retelling—it is an invitation into a divine adventure where God moves, speaks, heals, and transforms lives in ways only He can. But beneath every story is one invitation—an invitation I now extend to you.

This is not my journey alone. It is not reserved for ministers, missionaries, or those with extraordinary faith. It is for anyone who is hungry; anyone who is listening. Anyone who senses there must be more.

Along the way, you will discover that life with God is not meant to be lived at a distance. The Holy Spirit is not merely power; He is a Person. He speaks. He comforts. He guides. He delights in walking with us in the quiet moments just as much as in the extraordinary ones.

It is from that sacred place of awe and wonder that I share with you now. My prayer is that as you turn these pages, you too will encounter Him—not as an idea, not as a fleeting influence, but as the living Person of the Holy Spirit—the One who longs to fill you, flood you, and transform your life into the image of Jesus, God's Son.

Journey with me into the mighty adventures of the Holy Spirit—the One who reveals the Lord's great grace and power. Walk with me through stories of outstanding miracles, outpourings, and divine encounters.

Step into these moments as though you were there—feel the wind of His presence, hear the testimonies of His power, and let your faith rise.

Come along, my friend, and buckle up—the adventure with the Holy Spirit has only just begun. This isn't just a story; it's a holy adventure into the impossible. And perhaps, as this journey unfolds, you too will find yourself whispering the words that changed everything for me:

"I love You, Holy Spirit."

CHAPTER 1

The Night Heaven Interrupted My Plans

I will never forget the day my Aunt Lupi came waltzing into our family home like a whirlwind of ecstatic joy. She didn't simply enter the room—she filled it. Her presence was ablaze with delight, teeming with conviction, her every word charged with the joy of Heaven.

With that persuasive fire only she had, Aunt Lupi locked her eyes on me. Her smile radiated both love and certainty, and her voice carried a tender persuasion that made it hard—almost impossible—to resist.

"Anthony," she said, her voice brimming with passion that made my heart skip, "please come with us to see a woman whose ministry is filled with miracles and healings. Her name is Kathryn Kuhlman. Please—please—come with us. You will be so blessed."

To be honest, at 12 years old, it was the last thing I wanted to do. I was perfectly content in my familiar spot, happily settled into the comfort of an ordinary evening, watching my favourite sports program on television.

After all, it was the Dallas Cowboys playoffs! Why would I even think about leaving? But Aunt Lupi would not be denied. She pleaded, she persisted, and there was an urgency in her voice that made saying no nearly impossible. Before I knew it, I was dressed and climbing into the car, still wondering how on earth she had managed to convince me.

That car ride was unlike any other. Uncle Manuel drove focused, steady, and patient, while the rest of us talked excitedly about the service with Kathryn Kuhlman. Every word was filled with faith, looking forward to what great things the Lord would do that night.

Aunt Lupi's voice rang with expectation: "God is going to do something tonight. I can feel it!"

Her words ignited something in all of us—like fuel poured onto a waiting flame. My mother, Sara, was filled with a deep hunger for the things of God and the moving of the Holy Spirit. I could see that same expectancy alive in her eyes, reflected in the light of her face.

We all knew we weren't just heading to a meeting. Deep inside, it felt like a mission from God Himself. The air in that car was thick with anticipation, as though Heaven was moving us closer to a divine appointment.

When Heaven Filled the Room

When we arrived at the Houston Coliseum, I was stunned. The massive auditorium was already filling up—thousands of people pouring in from every direction, each face marked with hope and expectation. The room was dim, the air thick with quiet anticipation.

I remember standing there, trying to take it all in. *What is this? Why are all these people here? What are they waiting for?*

And then it happened.

Suddenly, the atmosphere erupted with the sound of a dynamic choir. A crescendo of voices rose in strength and power, unified and unstoppable. It was as if the very heavens had opened above us. The sound moved in waves through the coliseum, crashing over us with breathtaking glory. It was unlike anything I had ever heard. I can only imagine what Heaven must be like!

Then came an eruption of worship and wonder—Jesus, the King of Glory, had entered the room. Every heart bowed beneath the weight of His majesty as the choir lifted their anthem:

Then sings my soul, my Saviour God, to Thee,
How great Thou art, how great Thou art!

The sound filled every corner of the room—pure, reverent, alive with the glory of God.

My eyes were wide open, my heart racing. I was fully awake, caught up in the presence of God like never before. *What's happening? What is this?* I thought, overwhelmed by this unexpected encounter.

Then, suddenly, a single spotlight pierced the darkened auditorium and swept slowly across the platform. It stopped at the far left—and there she was: Kathryn Kuhlman. Her dazzling red hair framed her face, glowing like fire as she glided across the stage in a flowing, shimmering white gown. With every graceful step, the atmosphere grew stronger—alive, pulsing, charged with the presence of God. It was tangible.

Then—slowly, tenderly—the thunder of praise gave way to a hush. The glory didn't leave; it simply changed. The mighty roar became a gentle stillness, as though the Spirit of God Himself was now resting upon us. And from that holy silence, a softer melody rose—trembling, tender, unmistakably personal. The choir began to sing what I now know to be Kathryn Khulman's favourite song, "He Touched Me" by Bill Gaither.

He touched me! Oh, He touched me,
And oh, the joy that floods my soul!
Something happened and now I know, He touched me and made me whole.

The words wrapped around us with God's warmth—pure, radiant, overflowing love. You could feel the nearness of His heart, the gentle tenderness of His care for His people. I stood there undone, my heart burning, knowing deep within me that God was there.

The words rose from somewhere deep within—not rehearsed, not planned—just pure overflow.

I found myself whispering, almost shaking, "Yes, Lord, You touched me. And now I know—You've made me whole."

It was no longer just a song—it was my heart's confession, my soul's reply. In that stillness, I knew His touch had changed everything. He was here—so near, so real—and I was forever marked by His love. The atmosphere seemed to tremble with holiness, one of those sacred moments when you hardly dared to move. All you could do was sit in stillness, yielding to the gentle stirring of His presence.

Tears welled in many eyes as hearts melted before Him. The mighty roar of "How Great Thou Art" had declared His majesty, but now "He Touched Me" revealed His nearness—He wasn't just the God of glory above us, but the God who touched us, healed us, and made us whole.

Then suddenly—a pause.

A holy hush.

A sacred stillness fell over the great coliseum.

It was as though every breath became silent, and every sound surrendered to the presence of the Greater One who had entered the room. The atmosphere was pregnant with a heavenly pause. No music played. No one moved. Even the faintest whisper felt out of place. The hush carried weight—like the moment before dawn breaks, or the instant before a miracle unfolds.

Then, as Kathryn lifted her long, slender hands ever so gently toward Heaven, the presence of the Holy Spirit descended. It wasn't dramatic or forced—it was holy. A divine tenderness filled the air, moving like a reverent breeze across the thousands gathered.

People began to weep quietly. Some shook. Others simply closed their eyes, lost in worship. The reality of God's presence was undeniable—you could feel Him. Then Kathryn spoke again, her voice carrying the fragrance of Heaven: "Father God, we give You praise. Lord Jesus, we give You glory." She paused, taking a deep breath. "And we are grateful for the presence of the Holy Spirit here in this great coliseum."

Another pause. Then, measured and sincere, she said, "When I speak about the Holy Spirit, I want to go on record as saying—He is more real to me than any person seated in this vast coliseum." Her voice softened, trembling with awe. "He is so real...so very real—and He is moving, He is moving gently in this place. We give You praise."

Then suddenly, as if someone had switched on a divine light, miracles began to happen. It's hard to explain, but they started breaking out everywhere. People began testifying—blind eyes opening, deaf ears hearing, tumours vanishing, and bodies leaping with newfound strength. Wave after wave of rejoicing swept through the auditorium like holy fire, igniting every heart. Healing filled the atmosphere, saturating the air with unstoppable power.

Every shout of praise, every clap, every testimony became fuel for the fire until Heaven broke in, pouring through the room with divine electricity and the tangible glory of God.

And yet, amid the joy and celebration, a deeper stirring began to rise within me. Beyond the miracles unfolding before my eyes, the Holy Spirit was quietly touching my heart in a way that would mark me forever.

Just the Beginning

That night became the turning point—the spark that lit a flame in me that has never gone out. My life-changing encounter with the Person of the Holy Spirit took place at a Kathryn Kuhlman healing service at the Houston Coliseum.

What still amazes me is that I was only 12, but what happened that night I remember like it was yesterday, the turning point that set the course of my walk with the Holy Spirit forever.

But that first encounter was only the beginning. Something had been stirred in the depths of my heart—a holy awakening I couldn't fully explain. It was an unshakable hunger to know more of the Holy Spirit and to witness His mighty power. I longed to hear His voice again, to feel that same presence that had touched me so powerfully.

Little did I know, this was the opening chapter of a journey that would unfold far beyond anything I could have ever imagined.

CHAPTER 2

Where Hunger Became Encounter

By the time I turned 15, my life and my Sundays had been completely transformed. At exactly 9 p.m., everything else stopped. I would plant myself in front of the television, unshakably fixed on Kathryn Kuhlman's *I Believe in Miracles* program—week after week, drawn in as if Heaven itself had reserved that hour for me.

For two solid years, I listened as Mrs. Kuhlman spoke words of life, always pointing us to Jesus the Savior and to the sweet fellowship of the Holy Spirit, Whom she knew so well.

Even through the screen, I felt His nearness. That same warm, indescribable presence I had felt in Houston, Texas, as a young boy washed over me again. God's presence would meet me in my living room, as if the Spirit Himself was drawing me—preparing me for something I did not yet fully understand.

I don't have words to explain it. All I knew was that I had a Sunday evening appointment with the Holy Spirit, and the Lord was using His servant, Kathryn Kuhlman. Nothing could keep me from those broadcasts!

Then one night, unexpectedly, in the middle of her program, came an announcement: a group from Houston would be traveling to Kansas City to attend one of Kathryn's services in person.

My heart leapt—it felt as if destiny itself had knocked on my door. The excitement was beyond words; I was overwhelmed with joy! I wanted to go—I *would* go! All I needed was a miracle, and I knew God could provide it.

As it turned out, the Lord had already been preparing the way.

I was working after school as a janitor at the local bank, saving every hard-earned penny. At the time, I didn't think much of it—just a way to tuck a little money aside. But suddenly, all those hours and small wages had a purpose. I gathered everything I had and asked my parents for permission to go. To my amazement, after a long and determined conversation, they said yes.

Before long, I found myself boarding a plane full of hungry believers, each of us carrying the same expectation.

We were bound for Kansas City, heading straight into what would become one of the defining moments of my life.

AN UNEXPECTED AIRPLANE ENCOUNTER

There are moments in life that seem so ordinary—just another day, another journey—but later you realize Heaven had scripted every detail. That flight to Kansas City was one of those divine intersections, arranged by God long before I ever took my seat on that plane.

As I settled into my seat, still stirred by all that God had been doing in my life during that season, I found myself next to a family whose faces radiated warmth and quiet joy. At the time, I had no idea that God was about to turn an ordinary flight into a divine connection—one that would open a door to an amazing friendship.

We exchanged polite smiles, as travellers often do, and began to talk. To my amazement, I soon discovered that they were the wife and children of Captain John LeVrier, a Houston police officer I had read about in a Kathryn Kuhlman book I had devoured years earlier, entitled *Captain John LeVrier Believes in Miracles.* The very title of that book had once leapt off the page and into my heart. I had read it cover to cover, lingering over his testimony, inspired by the power of a God who still heals today. To my surprise, they, as a family, were on their way to the very same Kathryn Kuhlman meeting I was attending!

Captain John's story had marked me deeply. He had been diagnosed with stage-four terminal cancer and sent home to die. Every medical report declared it was over. Every doctor had given up hope. Yet, when all seemed lost, hope gave birth to faith.

Desperate for a miracle, Captain John travelled to attend one of Kathryn Kuhlman's healing services. He arrived frail, weak, and in constant pain—clinging to life and a fragile thread of hope. Unable to sit among the crowds below, he found a seat high in the balcony, longing for just one thing: to receive a touch from the Master.

Then it happened.

As the worship rose and Kathryn began to minister, the atmosphere shifted. The presence of Jesus filled the auditorium and surrounded Captain John like a warm, invisible blanket of liquid love and healing power. In an instant, the pain vanished. Every symptom disappeared. Strength surged back into his body, and he stood to his feet completely healed!

From that moment on, Captain John devoted his life to telling the world what God had done. He travelled across the United States, sharing his testimony at Full Gospel Businessmen's meetings and in countless churches, declaring the miracle-working power of Jesus Christ. Everywhere he went, faith was ignited, hope rekindled, and hearts stirred to believe again.

What an extraordinary man of God he was—and there

I was, sitting beside his family. Imagine that! They told me John himself hadn't been able to attend that evening due to other commitments.

I told them how deeply their father's testimony had touched my life, stirring a hunger to believe God for the impossible. They smiled gently and said, "When we return to Houston, we'll try to arrange for you to meet him." My heart leapt at their words, a thrill of holy anticipation rising within me. I could hardly contain myself. I had always longed to meet someone who had received a bona fide miracle!

As I sat there, I was overcome by the perfection of God's timing. What began as a commonplace flight had become a providential encounter in midair—a meeting only God could orchestrate. Was the Lord leading me into something new? Deep down, I knew He was. The God of miracles was revealing Himself—clear, near, and wonderfully real.

When we landed, my heart pounded with excitement. Each step off that plane felt like stepping into a story God had already written—one that would define the path of my calling for years to come.

It felt as if the Holy Spirit had whispered, *"This is where the next chapter begins."*

When the Impossible Became the Possible

From the outside, it appeared simple and unassuming, giving no hint of the glory within. But the moment I walked through the doors, I knew this was no ordinary place. The air itself was charged with faith, every breath alive with the possibility of a miracle.

Thousands filled the place—some eyes lifted in shining hope, others lowered beneath the heaviness of pain and need. Some sat in silence, carrying secret cries too deep for words. Yet in that vast crowd, a single thread wove us all together: a desperate longing for God to move.

The auditorium was massive—over 19,000 people crowded in. The air itself seemed alive, almost electric. I said it before, and I will say it again, it was as though the atmosphere was pregnant with miracles. You could almost reach up and take one. It showed in the whispered prayers, the silent tears, the low hum of faith filling the room. Anticipation was rising, like a great wave gathering strength, just about to break with power.

Being the curious adventurer that I was, I wandered over to the section reserved for the sick and disabled. My eyes slowly moved across the faces of those in suffering, each one carrying its own story of pain and waiting. Some lay on stretchers with IVs; others sat quietly in wheelchairs beside their chairs.

In that moment, as I took in the vast sea of needs, a quiet question rose in my heart—gentle yet piercing: *Will everyone here be healed today?*

That's when my eyes fell on a little boy—no more than

eight years old—restless, shifting in his seat as his mother tried gently but firmly to quiet him. His legs were bound in worn leather and metal braces, heavy and unforgiving. The sight gripped me, and my heart ached. *Lord,* I breathed within, *this child should be outside, running free, playing soccer, enjoying life like every other young boy his age.*

Moments later, a well of compassion rose within me, and I found myself praying for the little boy's healing. Suddenly, tears began to stream down my face—at first from my own emotion, but then something far deeper stirred within me, and I began to weep uncontrollably. In that moment, I became aware of something greater—an intercession not my own. *Who could this be, crying within, joining my tears with groanings too deep to understand?*

Finally, with quiet but earnest intensity, I whispered a simple prayer: *"Jesus, if You heal anyone today, please—heal this little boy."* Then, as swiftly as it had come, the burden lifted. A deep peace washed over me, and with a heart tender yet emptied, I quietly returned to my seat.

Moments later, the choir began to sing, their voices expanding until they seemed to shake the very rafters of the hall. The sound was electric and anointed, shaking the packed auditorium as worship surged like a mighty river toward Heaven.

Then came another one of Kathryn's favourite songs by Eugene L Clark, "Nothing Is Impossible."

Nothing is impossible when you put your trust in God
Nothing is impossible when you're trusting in his word
Hearken to the voice of God to thee
"Is there anything too hard for me?"
Then put your trust in God alone and rest upon his word
For ev'rything, O ev'rything!
Yes, ev'rything is possible with God!

Faith ignited like wildfire. Hearts lifted sky-high as the 500-voice mass choir thundered those faith-filled lyrics through the coliseum, every note echoing with the certainty that with God, truly nothing is impossible.

For those who never had the opportunity to be part of a Kathryn Kuhlman service, I want you to know that even though I was raised in a Spirit-filled, full-gospel singing church all my life, nothing could compare to the grace and anointing that flowed through Kathryn and her ministry. The music wasn't just inspiring—it was alive, charged with divine power.

Even now, my heart longs to see it again—to stand in mass stadiums once more, filled to overflowing with the glory and the power of God.

Then, almost slowly, the atmosphere began to shift. The thunder of worship softened into a holy stillness—a gentle calm that felt like the very breath of God resting upon us.

From that hush, the choir began softly to sing the timeless hymn by the Gaithers, *There's Something About That Name.*

Jesus, Jesus, Jesus; there's just something about that name.
Master, Savior, Jesus, like the fragrance after the rain;
Jesus, Jesus, Jesus, let all Heaven and earth proclaim
Kings and kingdoms will all pass away,
But there's something about that name.

Lost in the wonder of His goodness, Kathryn lifted her eyes toward Heaven. In that moment, we were reminded that He is not just the God of glory enthroned above us—He is the God who comes near. A holy stillness filled the room.

After a long pause, her voice broke the silence—pregnant with sincerity and fire. "I die a thousand deaths before I walk out on a platform," she said. "I don't care where it is, or how large or small the crowd may be. I die a thousand deaths because I know—better than anyone—that I have nothing to give you. I have no healing virtue. I have no power. You and I are completely dependent on the power of the Holy Spirit."

She lifted her hand slightly, her eyes searching heavenward. "Remember this moment. God the Father—the great Creator—is seated on His throne. I like to think of Him as the Big Boss. And at His right hand sits the great High Priest—the very Son of the living God. Everything we receive must come through Jesus."

Her tone softened, filled with wonder. “But here, in this place of worship, it is the Holy Spirit we honour—the very One whom Jesus trusted, the One to whom He offered Himself while here on earth in human form. The Holy Ghost—the mighty third Person of the Trinity—is here.”

The air grew heavy. You could sense Him moving through the crowd.

“I will not lay hands on you,” she said quietly. “You will come only after you have been healed.” Her eyes closed. Then, with a voice both fiery and full of reverence, she lifted her face toward Heaven and cried, “Move upon this people! We vow before the Father, before the Son, and before the Holy Spirit—to give You all the glory. We vow!”

For a moment, the entire coliseum stood still. Then, in a soft whisper that carried through the silence, she said, “Forget about Kathryn Kuhlman. Just close your eyes, and...” The words seemed to unlock something unseen. A hush fell across the crowd, and then—like a gentle but mighty wind—the presence of God began to move, thicker, heavier still.

Here and there, you could hear sobs, gasps, and shouts of joy as miracles began to unfold. And then, almost immediately, it began.

One testimony.

Then another.

And another.

Like sparks leaping into flame, miracles began to break

out across the auditorium. Diabetes vanished. Cancers dissolved. Tumors disappeared. Crutches were lifted high into the air as the crowd erupted in awe. Blind eyes opened. Wheelchairs emptied. Tears streamed down faces as healing swept through the room—touching, restoring, and setting people free. The presence of God was tangible—alive—moving like a holy fire that no one could contain. It rolled through the place with undeniable power, touching hearts and transforming lives in an instant.

Joyful cries filled the air as wave after wave of healing moved through the people. It was the miracle-working power of God—undeniable, unstoppable, radiant in glory—unfolding before our very eyes.

I stood in awe, hardly able to take it all in. My heart whispered, *How could anything be greater than this?* It felt as though I had just tasted Heaven on earth, and I knew within—I was the most blessed person alive!

It seemed only moments had passed while we were all caught up, raptured in His presence. Before long, it was evident the service was coming to an end, when suddenly, a stirring broke out to my left, moving swiftly down the aisle. Heads turned sharply as whispers rippled through the crowd. Every eye and ear was fixed on the stir coming down the aisle. Something was happening—something no one wanted to miss.

And then I saw him.

To my utter shock, wonder, and amazement, the very

same little crippled boy who had entered the meeting bound in heavy steel braces was now running—yes, *running*—down the aisle with all his might! Not limping. Not cautiously stepping. Running—full stride—as though years of captivity had shattered in a single moment.

The braces were gone. His legs moved freely—strong, steady, and sure—carrying him forward in a burst of unrestrained joy. His face shone with radiant light, his smile so wide it seemed to brighten the entire auditorium.

He wasn't just walking into freedom—he was discovering joy itself for the very first time.

And just a few steps behind him, another scene unfolded that gripped every heart. His parents followed, undone by what they were witnessing. They were weeping uncontrollably, tears streaming down their faces, their sobs raw and unrestrained, trying to catch up to their son, who was now nearly at the platform. They didn't care how they looked or who was watching—their cries told the story of a family overwhelmed by the sheer goodness of God.

I was wrecked. Awe and holy wonder swept over me, leaving me shaking in His presence. I knew without question that this was the hand of God. This was the touch of the Holy Spirit. That night marked me forever. Heaven's hand engraved something eternal upon my heart, igniting a fire that has never gone out—to be a vessel of the Holy Spirit, carrying Christ's healing, His hope, and His power to my generation.

When I walked out of that building, the world felt different—brighter, lighter, alive. It was as though my feet barely touched the ground. The Holy Spirit had filled every part of me, and deep within I knew I would never be the same.

Houston Bound

The next afternoon, I boarded my flight back to Houston, still wrapped in the afterglow of Heaven's touch. I carried no souvenirs in my hands, yet within my spirit burned something far greater—a living flame that no distance could quench.

My testimony was simple, yet life-changing: "That night lit a fire in me, and it has never dimmed."

When I returned home, I tried to tell my parents what had happened—to describe what I had seen, what I had felt, what I had encountered. But how do you describe the indescribable? How do you explain the miracles? How do you give language to glory? It felt as though my feet barely touched the ground. The Holy Spirit had filled every part of me, and I knew in my spirit that my life had been forever changed.

The Holy Spirit, who met me as a teenager in a crowded coliseum, did not leave me there. He walked with me through the years that followed—quietly shaping my heart, deepening my hunger, and teaching me to recognize His voice.

I came to understand that encounters are not destinations; they are invitations. Invitations to follow, to trust, and, in time, to go.

Long before I ever set foot in the Middle East, the Spirit was already preparing me—stretching my faith, loosening my grip on comfort, and awakening a love for people far beyond my own culture and nation. So when the call finally came, it did not feel foreign.

It felt familiar.

The same Presence that once filled a stadium would soon meet me again—this time in a small retreat centre near Bethlehem. And once more, the fire would fall.

CHAPTER 3

Israel:

A Call. A Confirmation. A Fire.

Some fires do not burn out—they deepen.

What God ignited in me as a teenager did not fade with time; it followed me quietly and patiently. Sometimes I could hardly name it—only that the Holy Spirit kept drawing me back to the same place: dependence.

Over the years, He trained my heart in ways I did not expect. Not only how to recognize His voice, but how to follow when He spoke—especially when what He asked didn't match what I imagined ministry would look like.

By the spring of 1990, that familiar stirring returned—only this time, it carried weight, full of direction. And it would come at a cost I did not yet understand.

I woke one morning with a pull toward Israel that made

no sense to my logical mind. I had never carried a longing to visit the Holy Land before, and it wasn't a dream I had pursued or a plan I had built. But that morning it felt as if a light had been switched on inside my spirit—and once it was on, I couldn't turn it off.

I didn't hear an audible voice. There was no dramatic sign. Just a steady, unmistakable knowing: *You must go.*

It surprised me how quickly obedience moved from idea to action. Not long after, I found a ministry tour while flipping through a Christian magazine and began preparing to join it. Even in those early steps, it felt like I wasn't *choosing* Israel as much as I was responding to a calling I didn't fully comprehend.

Just before leaving, a faithful man of God said something simple—almost in passing—yet it landed in my heart with deep significance: "Visit the Bethlehem Bible Centre."

I nodded, thanked him, and carried those words with me like a sealed letter, not yet opened.

Bethlehem

When the two-week tour ended, most people returned home.

I didn't.

Something in me wouldn't let the journey be finished. I extended my stay, determined not to miss the Bethlehem Bible Centre. I still couldn't explain the urgency—only that it was there, and it was strong.

When I arrived, I joined their worship for the first time, and the sound startled me in the most beautiful way. Arabic praise filled the room like a river, and I felt the atmosphere shift. There was a tenderness, a weight, a nearness that made my spirit go quiet inside.

My eyes drifted toward a window overlooking the rolling hills of Bethlehem. The view felt almost too sacred to take in with ordinary sight. This was the city of David—the fields where shepherds once kept watch, where Heaven's light had broken through the night with the Savior's star.

Then, without drama and without thunder, the Holy Spirit spoke. "Stay. Stay here and disciple My people."

It was so clear I almost looked around the room to see if anyone else had heard it. And then again, as if He knew my mind would try to dilute it, He repeated Himself. My heart trembled with awe, and my mind scrambled for a way to make it reasonable.

Stay? Here in Bethlehem? For how long? Lord, are You really calling me here?

I sat there quietly, the sounds of worship still echoing around me, as His words sank deep into my spirit. I knew that what had begun as a simple visit was now turning into something much greater. Heaven had spoken. The Holy Spirit was extending an invitation that would alter the course of my life forever.

And yet, if I'm honest, part of me wanted it to be a fleeting impression—something I could honour as a beautiful spiritual moment, but perhaps not need to obey.

But it wasn't fleeting. It was a real calling.

Afterward, I walked down to Shepherd's Field—the very place where angels once announced the Good News of Jesus' birth. The ground felt ancient under my feet, not as a tourist attraction, but as living history.

I sat alone and tried to breathe it all in. Bethlehem. The weight of Scripture. The wonder of God calling *me* to this place.

My heart swelled with awe and reverence as I whispered a prayer from the depths of my heart: *"Lord, I believe this was You speaking to me. I'm almost certain it was Your voice. But if You would be so kind, please make it clear that this truly is Your calling to Bethlehem. And when I return to the college for lunch with the faculty and staff, I ask that You would confirm it through the words of the president of the Bible school, so that I may know beyond doubt that it was truly You who spoke to my heart. Thank You, Lord. Amen."*

I remember standing up after that prayer, feeling both exposed and expectant, as if I had placed the whole moment in God's hands and now had no choice but to wait.

My mind swirling, I made my way back to the Bible school, where a feast had been prepared—falafels, olives, lamb stew—rich flavours filling the room with warmth. I sat at the table with my new Palestinian friends, faculty, and staff, smiling and making conversation, but my heart was listening for something else. We laughed, shared stories, and ate until we were content.

Finally, as everyone set down their silverware and the table grew quiet, the president of the Bible school took a deep breath and looked directly at me.

"Anthony, when you return to America, would you ask your pastor if he would be willing to release you to come and serve with us here in Bethlehem at the Bible centre? We would love to have you come."

For a moment, I couldn't speak. God had answered—word for word—through the very man I had named in my prayer. I sat there stunned. The One who called had now confirmed His word. In that moment, the fear didn't vanish, but certainty settled deeper than fear.

I knew, without question, that the Lord was sending me to Bethlehem to serve among the beautiful Palestinian people.

When I returned to the States, I shared everything with my pastor and family. With their prayers and blessing, I committed myself to the path the Lord had laid out—for what I assumed would be a season of full-time ministry.

Or so I thought.

The Paintbrush

A few months later, in September 1990, I was back in Israel. I arrived full of passion and calling...and was handed *a paintbrush.*

I didn't come as an evangelist reaching thousands or standing behind a pulpit. I came as a servant, assigned to help restore an old school building. The work was demanding, the days were long, the tasks repetitive. At first, it felt sacred. Each stroke of the brush felt like obedience—like preparation. But over time, fatigue seeped in. The work that once felt holy began to feel heavy.

My body ached. My spirit grew quiet in a way that didn't feel peaceful—I was weary. Questions surfaced that I didn't want to admit were there.

Is this really what You meant, Lord?

You called me to stay...to disciple...and here I am painting walls.

Did I misunderstand You?

One day, exhausted, I collapsed onto my bed and nudged the door shut with my foot. My eyes landed on something I had somehow never noticed before—a Christian poster hanging on the back of the door.

Bold letters stared back at me like a gentle confrontation:

> *"And let us not grow weary while doing good, for in due season we shall reap if we do not lose heart." (Galatians 6:9)*

I sat there and let the words sink in. It felt as if the Lord wasn't just speaking encouragement—He was forming something in me. What the world might call weakness,

God used as a doorway into deeper dependence—shaping me in ways no moment of success or achievement ever could.

An Open Door at Shepherd's Field

Not long after, the Lord opened a door in Beit Sahour—Shepherd's Field—the very place where I had asked Him for confirmation. A devoted woman of God had received a vision to reach local youth and began hosting Saturday morning gatherings. She invited me to join her.

On my first Saturday, more than 20 Palestinian teenagers packed into a small room. Their eyes were bright, their laughter quick, and their energy contagious. Yet beneath the youthful chatter, I sensed something deeper—a readiness I could feel in the room before I could explain it.

For three weeks, I preached Jesus to them. And one after another, they surrendered their lives to Him.

Standing there in Bethlehem, watching this simple harvest unfold, I felt as if the angels' ancient announcement was echoing again: *"Good news of great joy...for all people."*

As weeks turned into months, the youth group didn't just grow in numbers—they grew in fire. Their worship was pure, their prayers bold, and their hunger for God almost tangible. Each gathering carried a deep sense of anticipation—that something greater was on the horizon.

And then the idea came: "Let's take the youth on a retreat."

We chose a retreat centre called LeTron, about 50 miles outside Jerusalem. We prayed it would be more than an outing—that it would become a defining encounter.

On the day of the retreat, 30 young Palestinians arrived filled with anticipation. You could feel expectancy in the air—as if the hills themselves were waiting for Heaven to break through. I had come prepared with a message about the baptism of the Holy Spirit. It was burning inside me, ready to be released. But when the schedule unfolded, I learned it would be a local pastor preaching that session—not me.

For a moment, disappointment tugged at my heart. I didn't want to admit it, but I had pictured something else. I had imagined this would be *the* moment. The one where God would move through me, publicly, powerfully, unmistakably.

And right there, the Holy Spirit touched something tender inside me, not with shame, but with clarity. *"Will you let Me lead, even if you're not the one seen?"*

Revival, I was learning, does not come because we got the microphone. It comes when we surrender the need for it. A gentle peace washed over me—a quiet reminder that His ways are higher, and His timing always perfect.

Later, as the meeting continued, two young men quietly slipped out. Their posture told a silent story of deep discouragement, steps heavy with wounds from the past. An assistant noticed and leaned toward me: "Anthony, would you please go after them?"

I hesitated. This wasn't the "revival moment" I had imagined—no pulpit, no crowd leaning in, no wave sweeping through a room. Just two hurting young men walking away into the night. Yet in the quiet of my heart, I whispered, "Lord, if this is on Your heart, then it's on mine."

And Jesus' words rose in me like a call to surrender: *"If anyone desires to come after Me, let him deny himself, and take up his cross, and follow Me."* (Matthew 16:24)

So I followed.

I found the two of them walking along a quiet path, the weight of life written across their faces. Stepping closer, I put my arms around their shoulders and spoke words as tenderly as I could: "People may fail you, but Jesus never will."

The moment I spoke His name, I saw it—just a flicker at first, but real. Hope. A spark returning to eyes that had nearly gone dark. I slowed my pace and asked softly, "Have you received the Holy Spirit since you believed in Jesus?"

They glanced at each other, then back at me, and answered honestly: "No...we haven't."

"Would you like to?" I asked.

Their faces lifted. "Yes."

And in that instant, I knew Heaven was drawing near.

What happened next is forever etched in my memory.

It was as though a blazing torch ignited above my head—it was alive, twisting, dancing, and burning with holy fire. I knew instantly this was the presence of God.

The moment my hands touched theirs, it was as though a dam had broken wide open. Their mouths released a torrent of heavenly language, rising like a rushing river that could not be contained. Each breath carried more strength, more freedom, until their voices rang out into the night sky, echoing across the hills outside Jerusalem. As the sound of Heaven filled the earth, my heart was drawn to the Scriptures, and my mind went straight to the words of Acts 2:3–4:

> *"Then there appeared to them divided tongues, as of fire, and one sat upon each of them. And they were all filled with the Holy Spirit and began to speak with other tongues, as the Spirit gave them utterance."*

As their voices rose like a mighty river, I realized I was not merely recalling Scripture—I was standing in the very reality of it. Pentecost was no longer a story locked in the pages of history. It was alive, burning again before my very eyes. The same Spirit, the same fire, the same wonder resting now on two young men who had simply said yes to Jesus.

Then, another young man, unable to resist the sound, came running toward us. Breathless, wide-eyed, and eager, he blurted out, "Can I receive the Holy Spirit too?"

His urgency pierced my heart. The moment I laid my hands upon him, it was as though a surge of power arced from the top of my head to his. It felt like one candle bending low to light another, its flame passing gently, yet powerfully, from one to the next.

But that was just the spark before the fire began to spread. The youth came from every direction—some in twos, some in fours, others in small groups—until all 30 stood gathered before me. Their eyes glistened with wonder, their faces radiant with holy anticipation. I paused to explain what the Lord was doing and asked them plainly, "Do you want to receive the Holy Spirit?"

Without hesitation, every single one answered with a resounding yes. One by one, I placed my hands upon them, and the Spirit of God fell in undeniable power. Each young person was filled, and each voice broke forth in new tongues. The sound rose louder and louder until it became a mighty roar—an eruption of Heaven echoing across the hills of Israel.

In that sacred moment, deep within my spirit, I knew: the powers of darkness were trembling. Heaven's fire had broken through—and nothing on earth could stop it.

And then, something even greater began to happen. What had been a roar of tongues began to shift, almost seamlessly, into song. Their voices wove together—soprano, alto, tenor—each part rising and blending as though an unseen conductor was guiding every note. The melody bloomed, filling the air with a beauty so pure, like from another world, that I stood frozen in wonder. It was a holy choir unlike anything I had ever heard before—or since.

As the song slowly faded, another wave swept in. A deep spirit of intercession gripped the gathering. Some fell to their knees, tears streaming, others groaning with cries too deep for words. At least three young girls travailed in prayer, their voices breaking like mothers pleading for the lives of their own children.

Right there, before my very eyes, the words of Romans 8:26 came alive: *"Likewise the Spirit also helps in our weaknesses. For we do not know what we should pray for as we ought, but the Spirit Himself makes intercession for us with groanings which cannot be uttered."*

While the Holy Spirit was moving powerfully and the retreat grounds were alive with His presence, I noticed a man who had come with us to the retreat centre. He looked unsettled, his face marked by confusion and agitation. Suddenly, he rushed toward one of the young men who was praying fervently in his heavenly language. Gripping the young man's shoulders, he began to shake him, saying, "Halas! Halas!"—which in Arabic means "Enough! Enough!"—as if to pull him out of something he didn't understand.

But to his astonishment, the young man didn't stop. He continued to lift his voice, speaking in tongues with boldness and freedom. After a moment, the man's strength gave way. He lowered his hands, exhaled deeply, and simply surrendered. Sensing the moment, I stepped forward. Gently placing my hand upon his forehead, I began to pray. Instantly, the presence of God enveloped him. He lifted his hands as a new sound flowed from his lips—a beautiful, heavenly language that rose into the night air, echoing across the hills outside Jerusalem.

What began as a simple youth retreat became an upper room encounter—Heaven invaded, and a holy fire was kindled that no force on earth could extinguish. These young men and women were not just touched for a moment; they were marked for a lifetime.

The Spirit of God filled them with power, marked them with His presence, and prepared them for the trials that awaited. In that holy gathering, a generation was awakened—burning with the unshakable assurance that in Christ, the victory is already won.

As I stood among them, I realized the moment was shaping me as much as it was shaping them. I had come expecting to lead a retreat, but instead I was witnessing a move of God that would forever change my understanding of ministry. Watching these young men and women—faces radiant with glory, voices lifted in heavenly power—I knew I was seeing the hand of God write their destiny right before my eyes.

And in the quiet corners of my own heart, something

was sealed as well. I understood, perhaps more clearly than ever, that true revival is not something we manufacture—it is something God breathes. All He asks of us is to listen, to obey, and to carry His heart wherever He leads.

Lasting Impact

Word of the outpouring spread swiftly, as though it were carried on the very wind of the Spirit. Everywhere it went, it awakened curiosity and awe. For days, the young people could not stop praying in tongues. Even in their classrooms, the Spirit would fall afresh, and the heavenly language would rise like a song that could not be silenced.

Before long, the Orthodox priests gathered the youth and began questioning them about their experience. Bethlehem University itself was alive with reports—hallways buzzed with stories of what had happened at LeTron, and the sound of revival was on every tongue.

The stir became so widespread that even the city's leaders could not ignore it. Word of the outpouring reached the mayor of Bethlehem, and curiosity stirred his heart. Wanting to know more, he made his way to the Bible college to inquire about these remarkable events.

There, in the Bible school, the mayor was warmly welcomed and gently presented with the gospel. The Scriptures of Pentecost were opened before his eyes—how the Spirit fell in Jerusalem, how tongues of fire rested upon the disciples, and how ordinary men and women were clothed with extraordinary power.

The news could not be contained. It spilled beyond churches and schools, reaching even into political circles. Before long, word of the outpouring reached the PLO. Suspicious and unsettled, they began interrogating the young people, pressing them for answers. Harsh accusations followed—claims of Israeli collaboration, or whispers that they must have been under the influence of drugs or alcohol.

But no charge could hold. The joy on their faces, the boldness in their voices, the transformation in their lives—it could not be explained by anything human. Finally, in frustration, the officials relented, saying only, "Forget the whole thing."

But not everyone chose to dismiss it. Resistance rose swiftly. Graffiti began to stain the walls—mockery, slurs, and threats aimed at those who had been touched by the Spirit's fire. The very youth who only days earlier had radiated Heaven's glory now found themselves ridiculed, targeted, and even endangered simply for carrying the presence of God within them.

For my own safety, the president of the Bible school firmly urged me to leave Bethlehem at once, insisting that I go to Egypt until things settled down. And so, under his counsel and the Lord's leading, I was sent to Cairo for a season.

Leaving Bethlehem was one of the hardest decisions I had to make—my heart longed to stay with those young people whose lives had been so powerfully transformed. Yet even as I walked the streets of Egypt, I carried Bethlehem with me. The memories remained vivid: their worship rising like incense, tears of intercession soaking the ground, and the holy fire that had fallen upon them with undeniable power.

No threat, no war, no persecution could erase what God had done. What had been birthed in that hidden place was eternal—Heaven's imprint on a generation, a flame that no darkness could ever extinguish.

A Personal Outpouring

A generation was awakened that night, and their cry still echoes: "Come, Holy Spirit—come again!"

My friend, the same Holy Spirit who transformed those young people in Bethlehem, longs to touch your life too. He desires not only to visit you, but to dwell within you—to bring His peace, His power, and His holy fire. What He did for them, He desires to do for you.

Right now is your moment. Don't wait for another time. Wherever you are, lift this simple prayer from your heart:

> *"Lord Jesus, I open my heart to You. Fill me with Your Holy Spirit. Baptize me with Your fire. Transform my life, and use me for Your glory."*

Take some time to sit with the Lord and let Him do whatever He wants to do in these next few moments. I sense that some of you might start to cry, not quite understanding why. Maybe you feel overwhelming peace covering you, the weight almost like a blanket.

You might find yourself needing to lie down or kneel on the floor, receiving whatever the Spirit wants to give to you. Whatever it looks like, just yield. Don't rush. Let Him fill you. Whenever you're ready, take a few moments to sit quietly with these verses. Read them slowly. Let them soak into your spirit like living water. Pray them back to God and allow His Word to ignite fresh faith in your heart.

> *"'If anyone thirsts, let him come to Me and drink. He who believes in Me, as the Scripture has said, out of his heart will flow rivers of living water.'" (John 7:37–38)*

> *"If you then, being evil, know how to give good gifts to your children, how much more will your heavenly Father give the Holy Spirit to those who ask Him!" (Luke 11:13)*

> *"For the promise is to you and to your children, and to all who are afar off, as many as the Lord our God will call." (Acts 2:39)*

CHAPTER 4

The Miracle Worker in Bethlehem

The call of God does not always arrive in power; sometimes it comes clothed in surrender. When I came to Bethlehem, the Lord met me not in strength, but in weakness—and that encounter marked me forever. It was there, in the place where self-reliance fell away, that I learned His voice is often clearest when our own strength is laid down.

Among the Palestinian people, I began to glimpse the depth of the Lord's heart for His Church. I saw His longing for sons and daughters who would be filled with the Holy Spirit—not for display, but for devotion—empowered to carry His glory beyond familiar borders, into cities, nations, and ultimately, to the ends of the earth. What began as a personal encounter soon became a divine unveiling:

God was forming vessels of surrender through which His Spirit could move freely, bringing life wherever He was welcomed.

In that season, the Lord placed within me a clear and undeniable calling—to lead others into the baptism of the Holy Spirit, with the evidence of speaking in tongues.

I will never forget those days. Everywhere we went, something was stirring. You could feel it in the air—a deep, genuine hunger for God. The people weren't interested in theories or mere words; they were longing for something living—something real, something they could see, touch, and encounter for themselves. They wanted to experience the very power and presence they had read about in God's Word.

Compelled by the Spirit, I went from person to person with a holy urgency, asking the same question the Apostle Paul once asked the believers in Ephesus: *"Did you receive the Holy Spirit when you believed?"* (Acts 19:2)

To my amazement, many had not. Yet their hearts were wide open—tender, expectant, and ready to receive His fullness. Again and again, I watched as the Spirit of God descended upon the humble and the hungry—young Palestinian men and women, both young and old—until their faces radiated with God's light as His power came upon them.

Everywhere we went, the story was the same: His presence filled the room, and one by one, they were transformed from the inside out. As they lifted their hands in surrender, the Holy Spirit came— releasing power, joy, and freedom until it overflowed. Tongues broke forth like torrents of living water roaring before the throne. It was a spiritual eruption.

Hearts once bound by fear were filled with boldness. Voices once timid began to rise in praise, and sorrow turned into great joy. Heaven invaded the city of Bethlehem, igniting His people with the baptism of the Holy Spirit and fire. God was releasing His Spirit into the land—filling the beautiful Palestinian people with His power and presence.

Still, as I rejoiced in what God was doing, another reality began to press upon my heart. Living among the people, I could no longer ignore the immense needs of this ancient city. Everywhere I turned, I saw suffering written across the faces of those I knew the Lord loved.

I saw older women bent and weary from years of pain. Others struggled to walk, their bodies frail, spines curved, hands trembling under invisible burdens. Some carried large goiters in their necks, visible signs of long-suffering, untreated illness, and silent despair. The narrow streets of Bethlehem carried not only history, but humanity—groaning for healing, for relief, for hope.

My heart ached to see them healed and made whole. Yet in those moments, I felt the weight of my own limitation. I knew how to lead people into the baptism of the Holy Spirit—to see them filled with power and joy. But when it came to physical healing, I felt unprepared. I had no experience. No understanding. No faith grid.

I felt deeply inadequate. And so, like the disciples once cried to Jesus, I too prayed: *"Lord, teach us to pray."* (Luke 11:1)

As soon as the words left my mouth, I sensed His nearness. The atmosphere around me shifted—not in thunder or lightning, but in quiet assurance. It wasn't about how I felt; it was about who He is. A simple truth settled deep within my spirit like a stone sinking into still waters: Jesus Christ is the same yesterday, today, and forever. So if He healed then, He heals now.

How it happened or exactly *when*, I can't say. But what I do know is this—somewhere in that stillness, faith was born. Not loud but living. A spark that was ready to ignite into fire. Miracles, I realized, never begin with human ability; they begin with belief.

So, with tears streaming and conviction rising within me, I whispered, "Lord, I believe who You say You are—You are a Healer. You are a miracle worker!"

As I continued to wait on Him, in the stillness of prayer, the Lord placed a divine phrase in my heart that was so clear, so steady, I could not ignore it. It was simple, yet it carried undeniable weight. Day after day, almost without thinking, I found myself speaking it aloud:

"Jesus Christ is a miracle worker in the city of Bethlehem."

At first, it didn't feel like much. In fact, although my heart believed, I wasn't entirely sure my mind agreed. There was no surge of emotion, no dramatic encounter—just a quiet conviction that wouldn't let me go. So, even when I didn't feel like it, I said it anyway because deep down, that's what I believed.

I held onto those words, repeating them until they became woven into me. And as I did, the Scripture came alive: *"...faith comes by hearing, and hearing by the word of God."* (Romans 10:17)

Building Faith in Bethlehem

Little by little, something began to shift inside me. What started as mere words on my lips began to awaken faith deep in my spirit. It was as though God Himself was preparing me—laying a foundation for something far greater than I could see.

I didn't realize it then, but those simple daily declarations were not only for me—they were prophetic seeds. With each whisper, the Lord was planting faith for a miracle that would break forth in Bethlehem, one I had never dared to imagine I would witness.

So I kept declaring it, almost stubbornly, as I walked the narrow streets and bustling marketplaces. Past stone walls and crowded shops, I found myself breathing the words under my breath. Each repetition felt like an act of obedience: "Jesus Christ IS a miracle worker in the city of Bethlehem."

Weeks passed, but then, it happened all at once—something changed. As the words left my lips one day, it was as if God Himself breathed on them. Life filled the declaration. Fire surged within me. What once felt like routine repetition suddenly became alive:

> **"Jesus Christ IS a miracle worker in the city of Bethlehem! Yes, He is still the Healer today!"**

Later that day, the phone rang. I still remember the sound of it—sharp, unexpected, cutting through the stillness of the early morning. On the other end was a dear Palestinian brother, a man of faith and integrity. But something in his voice was different this time—tight, trembling, urgent.

"Anthony," he said, his words strained between breath and burden, "will you come? There is a woman here in town with her husband and two young boys. She is dying. Her heart is failing. She's on oxygen. Please...will you come and pray for her?"

The words struck me deeply. This was more than a request; Heaven was calling. This was the moment God had been preparing me for.

My heart began to pound as the weight of what lay ahead pressed hard against my chest. For a brief moment, doubt tried to creep in. *What if nothing happens? What if I pray, and nothing changes?* The thought hit hard, but I couldn't linger there. Deep within, another voice rose stronger, steady and sure: *This is what you've been declaring. This is what you've been believing for.*

Faith came alive in and through me, quiet but fierce, pushing fear aside. I took a breath, straightened up, and responded, "Yes, I will come. Let's go. I will pray."

SUHA'S MIRACLE

When I arrived at Suha's home, my heart sank. Two large oxygen tanks stood against the wall like silent witnesses to her struggle for life. She greeted me softly in broken English, her voice thin and her body frail. Her skin was pale and discoloured, every part of her showing how very unwell she was. Her husband and children stood close by, their faces marked with worry and uncertainty. Then, without warning, Suha whispered, "Look...see," as she lifted her nightgown to her knees.

What I saw left me stunned. Her legs were grotesquely swollen, nearly three times their normal size. Cracks had formed in her skin, and water seeped through the wounds—a clear sign that her kidneys had completely failed. In that moment, the weight of her condition pressed on all of us. Her body was shutting down before our very eyes.

In that moment, I realized Suha didn't need anyone's sympathy—she needed the intervention of God Himself. Everything in me knew this was beyond human help.

My heart raced as I gathered every ounce of faith I could muster. "Suha," I said gently, "I'm going to pray for you."

Closing my eyes, I felt the pounding of my heartbeat echo in my chest. This couldn't be any ordinary prayer—it would need to be a cry from the depths of my spirit. Faith rose within me, shaped by all the declarations I had been making in those quiet times of prayer, and the words came pouring out.

> *"Lord Jesus, You are the Miracle Worker in the city of Bethlehem. Suha needs You now. From the top of Suha's head to the soles of her feet, let Your healing power flow. Strengthen her body. Restore her life. Do what only You can do, Lord—and may Your name be glorified in the place. In Jesus' Name, Amen."*

To my surprise, when I opened my eyes, Suha was no longer standing in front of me—she was gone. Startled, I looked around the room, scanning every corner for her. My heart quickened as I turned toward her husband.

"Where did your wife go?" I asked.

He hesitated, his voice unsteady. "She...she went into the bathroom."

For a moment, we simply looked at one another—puzzled, uncertain, yet filled with quiet curiosity. Then, from the adjoining room, came the unmistakable sound of running water. We froze. Could it be? Was she truly strong enough to shower on her own? The thought seemed impossible after all she had endured. We exchanged glances of wonder, hardly daring to believe what we were hearing.

Ten long minutes passed before the bathroom door opened, and Suha stepped out. She wore a clean gown, but it wasn't her clothing that caught our attention—it was her. She walked toward us not weak, not pale, not dying, but radiant and full of life.

Still somewhat stunned, I asked, "What happened?"

With tears pouring down her cheeks, she said, "The moment you said, 'Jesus is a miracle worker,' all the water began to pour out of every pore in my body. I was soaking wet—and look at my legs now! Look!!"

We looked down, and her legs, once three times the size of her normal legs, swollen and cracked beyond recognition, were now completely normal—they were healed! The swelling had vanished. The draining had stopped, and her skin was smooth and whole. Every sign of kidney failure had disappeared—replaced with strength and life.

Her husband and children stood frozen, eyes wide with awe, unable to speak. We were all undone, completely overwhelmed by what we were witnessing.

This was no illusion and no exaggeration.

This wasn't emotion.

This was a miracle—undeniable and unexplainable.

Jesus Christ truly *is* the Miracle Worker in the city

of Bethlehem—and on that morning, He made Himself known. And the fire was only just beginning to spread.

Reflection: Let This Story Speak to You

My friend, I want you to pause for a moment and take this time to draw close to Him before moving on. He is always near; always waiting. This isn't just a story—it's an invitation.

Where do you need Jesus to reveal Himself as the Miracle Worker?

Is it in your body?

Your mind or emotions?

Your family?

A situation that feels too heavy to carry alone?

And let me gently ask you: **What fear has tried to silence your faith?**

Name it.

Bring it into His presence—not for shame, but for freedom.

He sees you. He knows you. He understands the weight you've been carrying.

Now consider this: **What simple declaration can you speak each day until faith awakens inside you?**

It doesn't have to be loud.

It doesn't have to be perfect.

It just needs to be honest.

Just as Suha stepped out of that bathroom transformed

by one touch from Jesus, ask your heart, **"What miracle am I believing the Lord for?"**

Write it down.

Speak it out.

Place it in His hands.

He honours faith—even when it begins as nothing more than a whisper.

The same Jesus who touched Suha is the same Jesus standing with you right now. His power has not changed. His compassion has not changed. What He did in Bethlehem, He desires to do in your life today.

Just as I quietly declared, "Jesus Christ is the Miracle Worker in the city of Bethlehem," you can declare: **"Jesus Christ is the Miracle Worker in my life today."**

Repeat it until faith rises.

Repeat it until your heart responds.

Repeat it until your spirit aligns with Heaven's truth.

Let this settle deep within you:

He healed then—He heals now.

He moved then—He moves now.

He came in power then—He comes in power now.

A Moment with Jesus

Before you move on, I want you to take another pause. Give the Lord this moment. Place your hand on the area that needs healing, or simply open your hands before Him.

Now pray slowly:

"Father God, I come to You in Jesus Your Son's mighty Name.
Holy Spirit, I welcome You.
Lord, release the same healing power in my life that touched Suha and transformed her.
Lord Jesus, I receive Your touch—
in my body, in my mind, and in my soul.
Jesus, You are the Miracle Worker in my life today."
Now declare by faith:
"I am healed.
I am strengthened.
I am restored.
The power of Jesus is flowing through me now."

Take a deep breath as His presence fills you and washes over you. Because this same Jesus is already writing your own personal miracle story.

CHAPTER 5

The Mountain Where Miracles Still Happen

The Mount of Olives has always felt like a place where Heaven meets earth. From its slopes, Jerusalem appears in a warm golden light—its stones glowing with prayer, prophecy, and promise. The air feels alive, as though every breeze carries the memory of sacred moments. The olive trees stand like living witnesses, their twisted branches holding stories of joy and sorrow.

This is the same hill where Jesus often came to pray, where He wept over Jerusalem. You can still trace His footsteps here. The atmosphere carries a sense of peace and purpose that words can barely describe.

But mixed within the beauty is also a quiet ache. The Mount of Olives is not only a place of glory—it's a place of suffering. It was here that Jesus prayed in agony in the Garden of Gethsemane, where His sweat became like drops of blood. It was here that He was betrayed, and from here that He ascended in triumph. Both pain and victory have left their mark on this mountain.

So when I was later asked to pray for a man in Mount Olives Hospital, something stirred within me. It felt like a holy thread pulling two moments together—ancient and present, sacred and personal. A sense of divine anticipation settled over me, as though the mountain itself was waiting once again.

God was about to write a new story of healing in the very place hope was born.

And even before I arrived, I could feel it rising within me—something was about to happen on that mountain.

The Man, The Mountain, The Miracle

Samir was a devoted husband and father of four. His life was humble and steady. Each morning, he opened the small souvenir shop he ran along the ancient streets of Bethlehem—serving pilgrims and travellers from all over the world.

Bethlehem buzzed with familiar sounds: merchants calling out their goods, families talking in the square, and visitors exploring its narrow lanes.

Samir's little shop sat tucked between stone walls along the old market road. Each day, people from around the world stepped through his doorway, searching for olive-wood carvings, candles, or hand-painted ceramics to carry home as memories of the Holy Land. Children often darted past the entrance, their laughter drifting through the cobbled alleys—blending the weight of history with the simple joys of everyday life.

Then, on an ordinary afternoon, the unthinkable happened. As I was later told, he had climbed a wooden ladder—something he had done countless times before—to reach a box high on a shelf. But that day, one small slip changed everything. The ladder shifted, and his balance faltered. In an instant, he fell backward, striking the back of his head on the stone floor below. The sound of the impact, they told me, thundered through the shop. Panic immediately erupted as workers and customers rushed forward, their voices breaking as they saw the severity of his head injuries.

An ambulance arrived within minutes, sirens wailing through the narrow streets as they rushed him toward Mount Olivet Hospital. To those who loved him, the city around them blurred into nothing—every second on that ride stretched into eternity.

What followed, as the family later described to me, felt like a nightmare unfolding in slow motion.

Hours passed in agonizing silence until at last, the doctor emerged—his expression heavy, slowly looking up to meet the eyes of the family. "I'm so sorry," he said quietly.

"There has been severe brain trauma. The damage is irreversible." The words hung in the air like a final judgement.

The man who had always been their strength now lay silent and unresponsive—his head wrapped in white sterile bandages, his eyes fixed in a blank, lifeless stare.

And yet, even in that moment when hope seemed lost, one fragile light still flickered: the hope of a miracle.

A Divine Assignment

I didn't know the man personally, but while visiting a woman of God in Beit-Sahour—a dear sister in Christ—I heard this heartbreaking story for the first time. As she finished telling me the story, her eyes filled with urgency.

"Brother Anthony," she said softly, "will you go and pray for him? Will you lay your hands upon him and believe God for a miracle?" Her words pierced my heart. I could feel the Spirit's prompting. This was no casual request—it was a divine assignment.

With quiet conviction rising in my spirit, I responded, "Of course I will. Let's trust the Lord together—He still does the impossible."

Making my way up the Mount of Olives in a taxi, I finally arrived at the hospital. When I stepped into his room—with a dear friend from Norway beside me—my heart sank. The man lay propped up in his bed, his head wrapped in thick white bandages. His eyes were open, yet vacant. He no longer recognized his wife, his children, or anyone standing near him. His family sat together on the couches, trying their best to hold a normal conversation despite the weight of their reality.

Meanwhile, he stared blankly above their heads—lost, disconnected from the world he once knew so well. There was no denying it—I was there on God's assignment. The moment I entered the room, I felt it. There was no need for small talk, no reason to delay. I had come for one purpose: to stand in the gap and lift this man before the throne of grace.

I turned to his wife and quietly asked if I might pray for him. Her eyes immediately filled with relief as she breathed out, "Yes, please—pray! We need the Lord's help."

Moved by the compassion of the Lord, I laid my hands upon him and lifted a simple yet fervent prayer.

> *"Father, in the Name of Jesus, I ask You to give this man a testimony for Your glory. Lord, raise him up from this bed and restore him to his wife and children. Let him return to his home, his work, and his family—fully healed, in Jesus' Name. Amen"*

It was not an elaborate prayer, but it came from the depths of my heart—spoken with the quiet assurance that the God of miracles had heard my request.

Then, as faith rose within me, I turned to the family and declared with conviction, "When this man is healed, I want you all to know that it was by the power of Jesus

Christ that he was made whole." They looked at me with wide, astonished eyes, unsure what to think. Yet behind their surprise, I sensed something stirring—an ember of faith, fragile but alive, reaching toward the promise of God.

I walked out of the hospital room with a quiet confidence in my heart. I had prayed. I had spoken what I believed. Now the outcome rested fully in the hands of the Lord. As I stepped outside into the cool Jerusalem air, I whispered a final prayer of thanks, trusting that Heaven had already begun to move on this man's behalf.

But almost as quickly as peace had settled over me, it was abruptly interrupted. As I climbed into an Arab taxi to leave the hospital, out of nowhere, I was suddenly struck with a sharp, searing pain in my left eye. It felt like some sort of terrible chemical had splashed into it.

"Lord, what is happening to my eye?" I cried aloud, pressing my hand hard against it. The pain was fierce—in fact, it was so intense that I could barely keep my composure in the back seat.

At first, I prayed simply for relief. But then, deep within, I knew. This was no ordinary pain. I believe the Holy Spirit revealed to me that what had happened in that hospital room had shaken the powers of darkness. A prayer of faith had been released, and God had begun to move. The enemy, furious at what had been set in motion, was striking back.

Even so, another truth rose stronger than the pain: the

victory was not mine to win—it already belonged to the Lord. The battle was His, and I could rest in that assurance.

So there, in that Jerusalem taxi—with tears streaming from my left eye and the fire of the Lord still burning within my spirit—I whispered through the pain, "Thank You, Jesus. You have heard. You will answer."

FORGOTTEN PRAYER, UNFORGETTABLE TESTIMONY

Shortly after the encounter at the hospital, I left Israel and journeyed across borders, preaching and ministering wherever God opened doors. In the swirl of travel, faces, and meetings, the memory of that man faded quietly into the background of my thoughts. I had prayed and moved on.

When I returned to Israel three months later, I stopped by to visit the friend who had first invited me to pray for this man at the Mount of Olives hospital. We sat together over tea, catching up on life and ministry. Then, in a flash, the memory came rushing back to me.

"By the way, whatever happened to that man—the one with the brain injury, the one the doctors said would never recover?" I asked.

Her face lit up with wonder instantly, a radiant smile breaking through. Leaning forward, looking deep into my eyes, she said, "You don't know?"

I shook my head. "No, I don't. Please tell me!"

"He got a testimony!" Her voice broke with excitement

as she shared. "Just one hour after you left that hospital room, everything changed. That man—who had been lying there lifeless—suddenly opened his eyes. He looked at his wife and children and recognized them all. From that moment on, he was fully conscious and alert. Within days, the doctors examined him again, and they could not believe what they saw. His brain was completely restored. His speech, his movement, his memory—everything returned. And before long, he walked out of the hospital and back home to his family, healed and whole!"

"Glory to God!" I erupted, tears forming and joy flooding my heart. Right there over that cup of tea, I was undone by the faithfulness of God. The Lord had done it!

"But that's not all," she continued, her voice filled with excitement. "Word spread like wildfire all around the area! It's been reported that over a thousand people from the surrounding villages came to witness what everyone is now calling 'the Bethlehem miracle'!"

Her eyes shone as she spoke. "They filled their little home wall to wall, people standing in doorways, crowding around windows, all trying to catch a glimpse of the man Heaven had raised."

As she shared, I could almost see it—faces lit with awe, neighbours whispering prayers of wonder, children tugging at their parents' sleeves, the sound of joy spilling through every corner of that humble home. "The whole region was talking. People couldn't stop saying, 'Jesus is alive! The power of God is real!'"

I later found out that his elderly mother—nearly 90 years old and living in Jordan—made the long journey across the border to see her son and witness his miracle. Truly remarkable.

What had once been a time of sorrow was now a time of thanksgiving. What had once been despair was now revival. The man's story had become a flame that could not be hidden. And deep in my spirit, I knew this was only the beginning.

"Lord, you did it. You gave him a testimony!"

We stood there in holy silence, aware that we were standing on ground touched by Heaven. No one needed to explain what had happened. We had seen it and felt it.

Jesus Christ had stepped into that small home in Bethlehem and done what only He can do. He had revealed Himself—not as an idea, not as a doctrine—but as the living Miracle Worker.

And in that moment, I knew this was only the beginning. The fire had found a place to rest, and it was ready to spread.

Walking by Faith, Not by Sight

Faith is often born in moments when everything around us says, "It's over."

That day at the Mount of Olives Hospital, nothing my natural eyes could see offered even a hint of hope. The man before me lay motionless, his body broken, his future gone. But faith does not ask permission from circumstances. Faith sees what God says, not what man sees.

So if you find yourself standing in a place that feels uncertain, take heart. If you have prayed and seen no visible change, keep believing. If you've wept in silence, wondering whether God has forgotten, He hasn't.

Faith means walking forward even when the road ahead is hidden. Faith is holding the promise when the only thing you have left is the Word of God burning quietly in your heart. The same power that raised that man from his hospital bed is still alive in you. The same Spirit that moved on the Mount of Olives is still moving in your home, your city, and your nation.

CHAPTER 6

Light Broke Through in Alexandria

Light has a way of announcing itself quietly at first.

When I arrived in Egypt, I didn't yet know that light was about to break through—in a church, in a young girl's eye, and in my own understanding of how simply God moves. I was new to Cairo, and every sound, every colour, every scent awakened something deep within me. The city moved with a rhythm all its own—vibrant, loud, and alive. The call to prayer drifted through the streets, weaving with the honking of taxis, vendors calling out their goods, and children laughing as they played. Everywhere I turned, Cairo pulsed with life.

The Nile cut through the heart of the city, its waters shimmering in the afternoon sun. Beyond the crowded streets, the Pyramids of Giza rose against the sky. The warm, dusty air carried a sense of history—something ancient and enduring—and I sensed the Lord's ongoing purposes for this land.

Cairo could be overwhelming at times, yet it stirred my spirit in a way I could not ignore. My senses were full—tired, yes, but alive with wonder at what God might do here. This was a place where prophets had walked, where Scripture had unfolded, and something new was beginning to rise within me.

I didn't know it then, but God was preparing to do something fresh—another release of His miracle-working hand in this land.

Not long after arriving, opportunities began to open. As a traveling evangelist, I was invited to different churches across the city. My message was simple and unchanging: Jesus saves, heals, and sets the captive free.

> *"The thief does not come except to steal, and to kill, and to destroy. I have come that they may have life, and that they may have it more abundantly." (John 10:10)*

> *"He Himself took our infirmities and bore our sicknesses." (Matthew 8:17)*

As I began sharing these truths among the beautiful Egyptian people—especially in the churches where I preached—I noticed something quietly shifting in the atmosphere. At first, it wasn't dramatic; it was subtle, like a gentle breeze of expectancy moving through the room. People leaned in with tender attentiveness, receiving every word as though it were water for thirsty hearts. Eyes softened. Spirits opened.

It felt as though a deep, generations-old longing was finally intersecting with the living Word. And in certain moments, it seemed the whole city paused—not because of me, but because of the simple, eternal message of a Savior who still heals today.

That atmosphere became even more tangible whenever I stepped out in faith and gave the invitation for healing. The response was immediate and overwhelming. There was no hesitation, no waiting for someone else to be first. Men and women, young and old, moved toward the front with urgency—as though they were running toward hope itself.

The line stretched across the altar and spilled into the aisles, filled with weary faces suddenly lit by a small, trembling spark of expectation. You could feel faith rising—fragile in some, bold in others, but unmistakably real—pulling on Heaven, reaching toward the One they had heard about but longed to encounter for themselves.

The atmosphere was thick with anticipation. Each person who stepped forward carried not only a sickness but a story—now meeting the living Christ. As always, I asked each one the same question, looking into their eyes and listening for the cry of their hearts: "What are you believing God for?"

I wanted to meet each person at the very point of their faith, to help them activate it personally—right there in that moment.

One particular night, I came across a young lady, perhaps 16 years old. She stood small among the crowd, but there was a quiet determination about her that drew my attention. Her face was bright, almost glowing with expectation, as though she had already seen her miracle before it came.

When I asked her what she was believing for, her words came with a steady, unwavering boldness. "I am blind in my left eye," she said softly. "The doctors here in Egypt told me there is no hope. They said if there were even the slightest chance, I would have to travel to England for a risky operation, and even then, they could not promise that I would see again. But I believe Jesus can heal me."

Her words stopped me in my tracks. For a moment, the room seemed to fade, and all I could see was her radiant, faith-filled face. I had prayed for many kinds of sickness before—fevers, tumours, arthritis, paralysis—but never for someone blind.

In that instant, a wave of inadequacy swept over me. To be honest, I didn't feel I had the faith to expect such a miracle. Yet, deep in my memory, a truth stirred in the form of a line I had once heard a preacher say: "Even if you feel your faith is small, honour the faith of the one who comes forward. God honours their faith too."

With that reminder, something shifted in me. Her faith shone brighter than my doubts, and her words carried a conviction that reached beyond my hesitation. I may have felt weak, but she stood strong—and I knew God was watching her.

I gently placed my hands over her eyes. My heart pounded, but I prayed as I would pray for any other seeker, declaring that *"By His stripes we are healed."* I stood on what God's Word said and came into agreement with it, and then, as quickly as I came to her, I moved on down the long line. Others were waiting, hungry for their miracle, and I pressed forward, laying hands, praying, and pouring out what I had to give. To me, it felt like so many other nights of ministry. I gave my best, whispered the promises of God, and placed the outcome in His hands.

But God was moved by this young girl's faith. What felt ordinary to me was extraordinary to her. What seemed like one more prayer in a long line of prayers became, for her, *the* prayer—the one she had held onto with all her heart, the one God had been waiting to answer. For me, it was simply another quiet step of obedience in serving the Lord. For her, it was the moment everything changed. And ultimately, it was destiny unfolding, a miracle already set in motion.

That night, while I walked away unaware, faith had

collided with the Word preached. The throne had heard, the Spirit had moved, and Heaven was already preparing to proclaim her story.

An Unexpected Reunion

After spending a few weeks ministering in Alexandria, Egypt, I decided to return to Cairo. Before I left, a friend asked if I would stop by the same church where I had recently preached, just to greet the pastors and encourage a few people who had been deeply touched during the services.

When I walked into the building, I barely had time to take in the room before a young lady came running toward me. Her face was lit with a mixture of urgency and joy—as if she had been waiting for this exact moment. It was clear she hadn't come merely to say hello; she had come to meet me for a specific reason. She was beaming, her smile wide and a bright ribbon tied in her hair.

"Pastor Anthony! Pastor Anthony! Do you remember me?" she exclaimed, her voice brimming with excitement.

I paused, taken off guard. Her energy was overwhelming, her joy contagious, but my mind searched for a memory I could not place. Finally, I smiled awkwardly and said, "I'm sorry, remind me—who are you?"

Her face lit up even brighter, and with joy spilling over, she declared, "I'm the young lady you prayed for—the one who was blind in my left eye!"

And that's when it all came rushing back. My heart leaped as I remembered the moment—the simple, trembling prayer, the quiet declaration of God's Word spoken in faith. I looked at her luminous face—eyes wide open, alive, and filled with light—and I knew. Heaven had moved. Jesus had done what only He could do.

Tears of joy streamed down her cheeks as she continued, her voice breaking under the weight of her testimony. "Pastor...the very next day after you prayed, I began to see light," she said, her hands shaking with excitement. "A soft, gentle light broke through the darkness! On the second day, I started seeing shadows moving—shapes, outlines, things I hadn't seen in so long. By the third day, I could see everything perfectly. It was clear, sharp, in living colour! Jesus healed me!"

Everything seemed to come to a standstill as her words hung in the air like a trumpet blast of victory. Faith ignited and awe swept over me as I realized once again: what may feel like just another prayer to us can be the very moment of breakthrough in God's timing.

To her, it was the miracle she had dared to believe for.

To me, it was a reminder of the mercy and power of Jesus.

And before the Lord, it became a testimony written into eternity, proclaiming to every generation: *Christ still heals today.*

Miracles rarely come wrapped in the dramatic. More often, God is already at work—quietly and gently—through a whispered prayer, a trembling step of obedience, or the simple faith of someone daring to believe Him. What happened in Egypt reminded me that God's power is not limited by our feelings, our adequacy, or even the strength of our faith. He responds to the heart that reaches toward Him in trust.

One prayer in Alexandria prepared the soil. One young girl's faith in Cairo opened the door. And God answered—not with noise or spectacle, but with a miracle that still speaks today.

So let this truth settle gently into your spirit: no prayer is ever wasted, no act of obedience goes unseen, and no place is too dark for His presence to enter. The same Jesus who healed in Cairo is still at work today, bringing light where there has been darkness and hope where there has been despair.

CHAPTER 7

"Jesus Wore My Neck Brace"

Some very close Palestinian friends from Bethlehem introduced me to a beautiful family who lived in the nearby town of Beit Jala—a name I had heard many times but had never visited until then.

Beit Jala rests quietly on a hillside beside Bethlehem. Its stone homes, narrow lanes, and olive trees give it a gentle, welcoming feel—slower than the busy streets below. You can sense history in the air, not because the town demands attention, but because it seems to carry the echoes of old stories.

Just beyond its borders lies the valley many believe to be the Valley of Elah—the place where David faced Goliath. Standing there, it's easy to imagine the young shepherd stepping forward with nothing but a sling, a stone, and a faith that shook a nation.

But on the day I arrived, my attention wasn't on the valley or the landscape. It was on the family I was about to meet. I didn't know it then, but the Lord was leading me into a story that would mark my life—and reveal His power in a way I would never forget.

It was there, in this quietly sacred hillside town, that I first met Basil and his family. The moment I stepped through their door, I felt it—an atmosphere of warmth and genuine hospitality that made me feel as though I had known them for years.

Basil carried a gentle humility, the kind that made you want to draw near. His wife, Rania, radiated a quiet strength and gracious kindness that instantly put me at ease. Their two young daughters darted in and out of the room, their eyes bright with innocent curiosity—filling the home with a joy only children can bring.

Basil had been in an accident years earlier that left him paralysed from the waist down. As they shared their story with me, I could feel both the weight they carried and the grace that sustained them. Over time, I found myself visiting often—sitting with Basil, encouraging him, praying with him, and believing together for the day God would restore what had been lost.

Rania carried her own quiet cross. As the sole provider for their family, she worked long shifts as a nurse at a hospital in Jerusalem, spending her days caring for the sick and injured, then returning home to care for her husband

and children. There was no complaint in her voice, only a resilient faith that held the family together.

One afternoon, I knocked on their door for what I thought would be a typical visit. When Rania opened it, she greeted me with her usual warm smile—yet something in her eyes told me this wasn't an ordinary day. As my gaze shifted, my heart sank. A medical brace wrapped tightly around her neck.

"What happened, Rania?" I asked softly.

Her smile faded into a tired sigh. "I was in a car accident," she said. "My neck is badly injured, and the pain is unbearable. I can't work right now, and I don't know what we're going to do. I'm the only one who provides for our family."

In that moment, the weight she had been carrying settled heavily in the room, and I knew this wasn't just a visit. I sensed the Holy Spirit stirring—something divine was beginning to unfold.

Knowing the gravity of their situation, I leaned in and said gently, "If you'll allow me, I would like to pray for you."

"Of course," she said, stepping aside to welcome me in. I placed my hand lightly on her shoulder and prayed a simple prayer of faith—nothing dramatic, nothing loud—just trusting that the Lord who sees and heals would touch her neck. Afterward, we shared a few minutes of warm conversation, and then I left, confident that God had heard.

The next day, I returned, eager to see what the Lord had

done. Rania greeted me at the door, smiling as always—but to my surprise, the brace was still there.

"You're still in pain?" I asked, disappointed.

"Yes," she said softly. "Very much."

For a moment, I searched her eyes—then felt faith gently steady me. "Well," I said with a small smile, "Jesus prayed twice. Let me pray for you again."

She nodded without hesitation. I prayed a second time—declaring God's promises over her body, speaking life and strength into her neck and spine. Afterward, we gathered with her family around their low table and shared a simple meal: warm za'atar bread, freshly pressed olive oil, and olives seasoned with lemon and herbs. It was classic Middle Eastern hospitality—comforting, familiar, and full of love.

On the third day, I returned once more. Still, the brace remained. Still, she was in pain.

This time, I felt a heaviness settle over my heart. Stepping aside near the doorway, I lowered my head, closed my eyes, and whispered beneath my breath, "Lord, I don't understand. Why hasn't she been healed?"

There was no voice. No thunder. No explanation. Only a quiet assurance resting deep within me, urging me to trust Him. I did not pray again that day. Instead, I placed her gently into His hands, trusting, even though I did not understand.

He Took My Pain, Too

Two days later, I decided to visit again—this time, not expecting much, only wanting to share fellowship and encouragement. When Rania opened the door, I froze. Her face was vibrant, gleaming with joy. But that wasn't what stunned me—it was her neck.

The brace was gone.

"What happened?" I asked, eyes wide. "Are you healed?"

She laughed softly, her smile stretching with delight. "Yes, I am healed—but no thanks to you," she teased lovingly. "Come in, and I'll tell you what happened."

As we sat at the table, Rania began to speak with tears in her eyes. "Last night," she said, "I had a dream. I found myself standing at the base of a hill covered in rubble. When I looked up, I realized it was Calvary—the place where Jesus was crucified.

"I saw Him hanging there on the cross, and I was shocked by what I saw. Anthony, He was so beaten, so crushed, that it was hard to even recognize Him as a man. The sight broke me. I fell to the ground, burying my face in the dirt, and I began to weep uncontrollably. I cried because I knew it was my sin that had put Him there.

"I wept and wept until I had no strength left. Then, for some reason, I lifted my head and looked again at Jesus on the cross. It was still Him—bruised, bleeding, suffering—but something was different this time."

I leaned in. "What did you see, Rania?"

She took a breath. "Anthony...He was wearing my neck brace."

Her words gripped me. She continued through tears, "When I saw Him wearing it, I understood. I saw it clearly. Jesus didn't just go to the cross for my sins; He took my pain, too. He carried my sickness, my suffering, my injury. He bore it in His body. He was wearing my brace because He had taken my pain."

She smiled through tears. "When I woke up, I realized I was healed. The pain was gone. I took off the brace and could move freely. Jesus took both my sin and my sickness on the cross. He paid the price for *all* of it."

As she spoke, I felt the presence of God fill that small room. Her words echoed the Scripture itself: *"He Himself took our infirmities and bore our sicknesses."* (Matthew 8:17)

Jesus not only bore our sins but also our sicknesses. The cross was complete. Redemption was not partial; it was total. Rania had seen what many believers struggle to grasp—the finished work of the cross. What Jesus bore, we do not have to carry. What He suffered, we do not have to endure. He took it all, our sin, sickness, pain, and sorrow and nailed it to the cross.

That day, I left their home overwhelmed. The Lord had used a dream—a personal revelation—to heal a devoted wife and mother, and to remind me of a truth eternal: It is finished. Healing flows from the same fountain as forgiveness. Both were purchased at Calvary.

When we see what He carried, we understand what we are free from. When we behold the suffering of the Savior, we recognize the depth of His love—and the completeness of His work.

REFLECTION: JESUS CARRIED IT ALL FOR YOU

Before going to the next chapter, I want to pause again for a moment. Take a breath and acknowledge the Lord's Presence and invite Him to fill your heart right now.

Let this story speak to you personally.

What part of Rania's dream reached you the deepest? Was it the weight of the pain she saw on the Lord's face? Or the moment she realized that Jesus Himself had already carried every ounce of it for her? How does her story reshape the way you see the cross today?

The cross is not only the place where Jesus forgave your sins—it is the place where He carried every sorrow, every wound, every fear, every hidden burden you were never meant to bear.

So let me gently ask you:

What "neck brace" are you still wearing?

What pain still lingers?

What fear still whispers?

What memory still weighs on your heart?

What burden have you been carrying in silence?

And what would change in your life if you saw—just as Suhaila did—that Jesus has *already taken it*?

He didn't ask you to carry it. He carried it for you.

Let the Holy Spirit speak softly to your heart: "You don't have to hold this anymore. Jesus has lifted it from your shoulders to His and has removed it far away."

After you've spent some time pondering and reflecting on the questions, I want you to pray this aloud:

> *"Lord Jesus, thank You for the cross—for bearing not only my sin, but my pain, my sickness, my fear, and every hidden burden I've carried in my heart. Open my eyes as You opened Rania's. Help me see what You have already carried for me.*
>
> *Where I have held on to fear, heal me. Where I have carried sorrow, lift it from me. Where my heart has grown weary, breathe new strength into me.*
>
> *Teach me to trust Your finished work. Teach me to rest in Your victory. Let Your healing presence flow through my mind, my emotions, and my body.*
>
> *I receive Your peace.*
>
> *I receive Your healing.*
>
> *I receive the miracle You have for me.*
>
> *And I declare by faith: It is finished. Jesus has done it all for me. Thank you, Lord, I am healed and set free!"*

CHAPTER 8

From Dust to Snow to Fire

I didn't know it then, but my life was about to turn in a direction I never expected—one that would carry me from the dusty streets of Israel to the snowy landscapes of Sweden, and eventually to a secluded island in the Mediterranean. There, I would walk alongside and equip young Arabic men who had encountered Jesus. It was a season of divine redirection, of God gently yet firmly shifting my steps according to a purpose only He could see.

It began in Israel.

I was serving among the Palestinian people, witnessing the Holy Spirit baptize many with fire and heal the broken in ways that left me in awe. In the midst of that season, I met an apostolic minister from Sweden who was touring the land with his church team. Our meeting was unplanned—divinely arranged, really. Someone who knew him felt prompted to suggest we meet, and within a day, I found myself sitting across from him and his wife in the hotel café, having coffee and sharing all the awesome testimonies of what the Lord had been doing.

As I poured out my heart—my love for the Palestinian people, the salvations, the healings, the baptisms in the Spirit—he listened intently, visibly moved. And then, almost out of nowhere, he leaned forward and spoke words I never expected to hear.

"Anthony," he said with a sincerity that caught my attention, "we have a tremendous Bible school in Sweden, and I believe with all my heart that God has a purpose in mind for you there. I would like you to consider coming for a full year to study, to grow, and to deepen your personal walk of faith. I want to offer you a full scholarship and a place to stay. Will you pray about this? I truly believe you will be greatly blessed."

I was stunned. I had sensed a transition was coming—yes—but *Sweden?* Bible school? Snow, a new culture, a foreign language, and a world so completely different from the Middle East? Nothing about it made sense in the natural, and yet, deep down, a quiet excitement and wonder began to stir.

For years, my heart had been rooted in Israel. My ministry was flourishing among the Palestinian people. Everything was familiar—every friendship, every routine, every breakthrough was happening there. That was my world.

And yet, almost out of nowhere, Sweden stepped into the story.

There was a weight on this invitation—a gentle authority that did not feel human. Something in my spirit recognized that this might very well be God.

So I took it to prayer. Day after day, over the weeks that followed, I laid it before the Lord. And slowly, the confirmations began to come—clear, specific, and far beyond coincidence. It became harder and harder to call it "just an opportunity." In my heart, I knew: This was a divine invitation. And if I said yes, my life would never be the same.

I was visiting a close friend—one who moved strongly in the prophetic—when, without warning, he shared something the Lord had shown him in prayer. He described a vision of a map of the Middle East, and suddenly a red arrow shot from Israel across to Europe, landing on the nation of Sweden. He felt strongly that it had something to do with me.

I sat there, stunned, because in that instant I knew the Lord was confirming the invitation I had told *no one* about. Only God knew.

My friend looked at me and said slowly, "Anthony, I see you being transported from Israel to Sweden. I don't know where or why—but that's what I see."

I froze. Something leapt inside my spirit—a holy certainty, a quiet knowing, a sense of divine alignment so strong it nearly took my breath away.

God wasn't just opening a new season—He was redirecting my destiny.

A New Beginning in Sweden

Months later, I found myself in Uppsala, Sweden—stepping onto the grounds of a Bible school that would shape the next season of my life. Only a short time earlier, I had been walking the streets of Jerusalem; now I was in the chill of Northern Europe, surrounded by students burning with hunger for God. And just as I did, many sensed that something historic was beginning to stir across the nations.

Revival winds were blowing.

During those first months of that unforgettable year—with more than 500 international students gathered in my class—the work of the Lord in me and through me was remarkable. Nations were being etched deeper into my heart as my studies were enriching my spirit, and my vision was widening with every passing week. I didn't know it then, but the Lord was using that season to prepare me for the next step in the unfolding story of His calling on my life.

I remember the wave of excitement that swept through our Swedish church and Bible school when we heard that a man of God—a pioneer of a mighty work in the Middle East—was coming to speak. The news spread quickly among the students. Conversations erupted in the hallways as reports circulated of a powerful move of the Holy Spirit taking place through his ministry.

This wasn't just another guest speaker. We had heard that the Lord was using this minister to break through some of the hardest spiritual soil on earth—and his stories sounded like the book of Acts unfolding in real time.

We were all eager, stirred, and full of expectation.

When the guest speaker finally arrived in Sweden, and the long-awaited evening came, the church was already overflowing. Students, pastors, and families arrived early and packed in. Even the aisles and walls were lined with hungry hearts.

The moment he stepped onto the platform, the atmosphere shifted. There were no theatrics—just the quiet authority of a man carrying Heaven's assignment. He began sharing his bold new vision: a satellite outreach across the Middle East unlike anything ever attempted.

"Introduce Yourself to Him"

As he spoke, it felt as though we were being pulled straight into the heartbeat of God's purposes. He described homes across the region quietly tuning in—families gathering secretly around their televisions, keeping the volume low so neighbours wouldn't hear—to what their hearts had longed for their whole lives.

The Holy Spirit was moving. Healing. Saving. Transforming.

He shared that entire villages were hearing the gospel for the very first time, and the Word of God was breaking into places long closed to the light. Story after story poured out of him—each more astonishing than the last.

For many viewers, he explained, this was the first time in history they had ever heard the full gospel preached in Arabic—clearly, boldly, and without compromise. Night after night, the message of Jesus was reaching places no preacher could ever walk into. And lives were being changed.

Then he paused, lowered his voice slightly, and said, "And that's when the miracles began."

He explained that at first, just a few testimonies trickled in, but soon they multiplied.

Deaf ears opening.

Blind eyes seeing.

Cancer disappearing.

Families freed from long-standing afflictions.

Marriages restored.

Sons and daughters coming home.

One story after another, each one carrying the unmistakable fingerprint of God.

"What started as a broadcast," he explained, "became a movement of miracles and salvations. What began as a programme ignited into a fire. The letters started coming. First a few, then dozens, then more than anyone could physically count."

"I was healed."

"Jesus came into my heart."

"What do I do now?"

These weren't just letters—they were cries of newborn faith. Stacks of envelopes filled his office. He said the weight of it often drove him to his knees—praying, weeping, asking God for direction.

"And that," he said softly, pausing as if remembering the exact moment in real time, "is when everything changed. One night, while I was praying on the floor, I heard the Holy Spirit speak so clearly."

He paused again, letting the moment settle, then repeated the words slowly—almost reverently:

"'Establish a hidden Bible school. Bring them in. Train them in My Word. Let them encounter My Spirit.'"

It was bold, dangerous, and utterly impossible. But the moment he spoke it, we all felt the fire of God. This was no man-made plan. This was God-breathed—Heaven's whisper breaking into earth's impossibilities. When the Lord releases a word, nothing can stop what He intends to build.

As he continued speaking to the church that night, a glorious heaviness settled over the room—the kind that only comes when God Himself is speaking through a man.

"There is an island," he said slowly, "a place called Cyprus. It is a land once walked by Paul, Barnabas, and Mark as they carried the gospel to the nations. And now that same island is becoming a doorway for a new move of God."

Everyone leaned in, sensing the magnitude of what he was unveiling.

"The Lord has placed a burden on my heart," he continued, "to establish a hidden Bible centre there—a safe place for former Muslims who have come to Christ through dreams, visions, and the satellite preaching of the gospel. These young men cannot return to their home nations without risking their lives. But in Cyprus, we can disciple them, equip them, and send them into regions where missionaries cannot go."

His eyes burned with conviction.

"This will be one of the most unique and strategic training centres we have ever attempted—a place where the fire of the early church meets the harvest of the last days."

As he preached, something I couldn't explain stirred deep within me. His message came straight from the heart, carrying the weight of a heavenly mandate—to reach the Arab world with the gospel through satellite television. He spoke of a short window of time the Lord had impressed upon him, a divine urgency to train, equip, and send out those who had once walked in darkness but were now burning with the light of Christ.

It was an invitation wrapped in a mandate. And that night, we realized that each of us had a part to play in the story the Lord was writing.

Near the end of that fiery gospel message, something utterly life-changing happened. In the midst of the passion, the vision, and the weight of Heaven in the room, I heard a gentle whisper rise within my spirit—clear and filled with purpose: "Anthony, go and introduce yourself to this man."

I froze. *Did I really hear that? Was that the Lord?* For a moment, I brushed it aside—maybe it was just my own thought. But then the voice returned, clearer, stronger, unmistakably His: "Anthony, I want you to go and introduce yourself to this man."

I hesitated again, unsure, wrestling inside. Then the word of the Lord came a third time—this time with a loving but firm correction: **"I said, 'Go and introduce yourself to him.'"**

That settled it. No more questions. No more delay.

I jumped to my feet, fully aware of how difficult it would be to get anywhere near this guest speaker after such a powerful service. Three ushers and a security guard formed a clear wall between the platform and the congregation. Still, obedience burned in my heart—I had to go.

As I approached the first usher, her back was turned. Then suddenly, as if mandated by Heaven, she spun around. Her eyes locked onto mine with intensity, as though she already knew my purpose. Gripping my hand, she said urgently, "You must meet this man!"

Before I could respond, she pulled me past the other ushers and the guard—straight to the front. Within seconds, I was standing at the foot of the platform, looking up into the eyes of the servant of the Lord I had been commanded to meet.

He looked at me, somewhat bewildered, as if to say,

"Yes? How can I help you?" Gathering my courage, I spoke quickly, "I'm very, very excited about all that you shared today—particularly about the training school in Cyprus for the young men who have come to Christ. This is wonderful!"

To my surprise, his demeanour changed. He seemed to shrink back, fear flickering in his expression. With a hushed urgency, he said, "Whatever you do, do *not* tell anyone about this Bible centre. Keep it to yourself, please. I don't want this to be spread around!"

I was taken aback. I had obeyed the Lord's prompting, but his reaction left me unsettled, almost as though I had overstepped. On my way back to my seat, I carried a strange mixture of emotions: a quiet joy in obeying God, yet confusion over the response I had received.

The next morning, I got up early, still unsure what to make of everything that had happened the night before. I decided simply to give it back to the Lord and trust Him with it. After getting ready, I went to our regular morning Bible school sessions. Once again, our guest from the Middle East was scheduled to preach.

His preaching moved us deeply, stirring hearts from every corner of the world. After the class ended, the room buzzed with conversation as we filed out. I had barely begun speaking to a friend beside me when a sudden voice pierced through the chatter, calling my name: "Anthony! Come here—I want to talk to you!"

I froze. Surely he didn't mean me. Not after yesterday. Not after the awkward exchange and his fearful reaction.

But then he called again—this time sharper and undeniable: "Anthony, I'm talking to you. Come here, please."

My heart tightened as I made my way toward the pulpit, a strange mixture of caution, curiosity, and wonder rising inside me. He kept his eyes on me the whole time—serious, focused, almost searching. When I reached him, he leaned in and spoke quietly, but with a weight that made the room feel still.

"This morning, while I was in prayer, your face came before me. And the Holy Spirit said to me, 'You will be the dean of the Bible school in Cyprus—for Me.'"

I stood there stunned.

As those words landed, something deep inside me clicked—like a key turning in the lock of my destiny. A quiet certainty rose in my spirit, the kind no man can manufacture. My eyes filled with tears. I could barely speak, but I managed to whisper, "Wow, okay. Thank you."

He reached into his pocket, pulled out a small piece of paper, and pressed it into my hand.

"Contact me when I return to the States," he said gently. "We'll talk more."

I walked back to my seat in a daze, the presence of God resting on me like a warm, steadying hand. Something had shifted. Something holy and irreversible.

All of a sudden, I knew—I hadn't misunderstood His

voice. The call to Cyprus was real. And it wasn't just about me. It was for the men who would one day come: young men from the Arab world transformed by the love of Jesus, trained, equipped, and empowered to carry the gospel into places missionaries could never go.

This wasn't just another assignment. It was the beginning of something far bigger—a divine spark that would ignite revival on that island and far beyond.

What an amazing God we serve.

He sees the hidden desires we never speak, the quiet longings of our hearts, and in His perfect timing, He weaves them into His story. He takes simple obedience and turns it into divine appointments. He breathes purpose into moments that seem small and ordinary until they carry the power to shape lives, influence nations, and echo into eternity. This is the God who goes before us, who orders our steps, opens doors no one can shut, and turns obedience into destiny.

From that day on, the vision for the island training centre burned within me. A new chapter had begun—one I never planned or expected, yet one Heaven had written long before I ever knew it existed.

Where the Breath of God Fell

High in the rugged mountains of the island of Cyprus stood an abandoned sanatorium—once a tuberculosis centre, marked by sickness, fear, and quiet suffering. To most, it was nothing more than a forgotten shell, worn down by time and history.

But to God, it was something entirely different. It had been set apart.

What once held the breath of disease would soon hold the breath of Heaven. The Holy Spirit was preparing to breathe life into the spiritual lungs of young men who had stepped out of darkness and into the light of Christ.

> *"So I prophesied as He commanded me, and breath came into them, and they lived, and stood on their feet, an exceedingly great army." (Ezekiel 37:10)*

This unlikely mountain refuge had been chosen to become a furnace of training—a place where once-silent voices would rise with boldness, where timid hearts would be shaped into courageous witnesses for Jesus. I still remember the first time I walked through its forgotten halls. Dust drifted through beams of sunlight that spilled across broken windows. Everything was still—almost eerily so—yet the quiet carried a deep sense of expectancy, as though time itself had paused, waiting for God to write a new chapter.

In that silence, the Lord spoke clearly to my heart: "This place is Mine."

A holy awe settled over me. I knew Heaven was laying

claim to this ground as Joel's ancient prophecy rose within my spirit like a fresh flame: *"I will pour out My Spirit on all flesh..."* (Joel 2:28)

This was not merely a building; it was a fulfillment already set in motion.

Through divine connections I could never have orchestrated, I was appointed as the first dean of the training centre. I arrived with no titles, no accolades—just an open heart. Yet God took that simple yes and wove it seamlessly into His unfolding plan.

Looking back now, I can see His fingerprints on every detail. This had never been an abandoned sanatorium. It was a stage God had been preparing for years—quietly, patiently—waiting for the moment the Holy Spirit would breathe upon it again.

Purpose and Power Revealed

The vision was simple yet carried eternal weight: to host a three-month training course designed to ground these young believers in the Word while leading them into a life-changing encounter with Jesus through the power of the Holy Spirit. From that moment on, my prayer became both constant and clear: "Father, may they meet You, Your Son, and Your Spirit in a personal way."

And Heaven answered.

One by one, young men from Jordan, Israel, Morocco, Egypt, and beyond arrived, each carrying their own life story. They arrived quietly, almost unnoticed, as if drawn by the gentle leading of the Holy Spirit.

Many travelled under the cover of night, crossing guarded borders and whispering prayers as they went. For many, stepping into the Good News Bible Centre required a level of courage that could cost them everything. This was not a small decision nor merely a change of beliefs; it was surrender. They risked exposure, rejection, imprisonment, and even death. Their presence had to remain hidden from families, neighbours, and entire communities. Some had been scholars of their former faith—trained to become future leaders. Yet they came, not out of curiosity, but because they had encountered God's Presence they could not deny. A Voice greater than fear had called them.

Behind those guarded walls, Heaven began to write new stories. It was more than a school—it became an altar. Every prayer, every tear, every surrender became fuel for a coming revival that would one day touch nations.

What unfolded within those halls went far beyond teaching—it was transformation. What began quietly soon grew into a move of God that could not be contained. These young men, once hesitant and wounded, were ignited with holy fire. Their prayers carried weight. Their worship rose pure and unrestrained. Their testimonies began to stir faith in all who heard. Hope awakened, and hearts were set ablaze with love for Jesus. The rooms that once echoed with sickness and silence now overflowed with fiery intercession, joyful laughter, and the sound of redemption breaking chains.

What had once been a hidden refuge had become a furnace of divine encounter—a place where the Holy Spirit broke chains, healed wounds, and rewrote destinies. By day, we watched faith awaken, and night after night, we watched Jesus reveal Himself in ways only He could.

These were not students merely learning doctrine—they were sons discovering their Father. And nothing would ever be the same again.

As the days unfolded, a familiar stirring rose within me—the same burden I had carried in Bethlehem: to teach and impart the fullness of the baptism of the Holy Spirit during each three-month session. And just as I had witnessed among the Palestinian believers, these young men from the Middle East yielded themselves with remarkable purity and hunger.

What happened next could only be described as supernatural.

Classroom after classroom, session after session, across two unforgettable years, the Holy Spirit came. I watched as they were reshaped, day after day, into the image of Christ. They were filled, then refilled—overflowing with His Spirit until knowledge gave way to lasting change. They left not merely informed but ignited—carrying within them a divine commission stamped by Heaven. I knew they would not remain on that mountain forever. This fire was not meant to be contained. It would spread into cities where darkness ruled, villages where hope was scarce, and nations long resistant to the gospel. They would go as living torches—of His glory carried by willing hearts.

What made this Training Centre so extraordinary was that Jesus wasn't limited to the classroom or the daylight hours—He made Himself known among us. It wasn't only through the teaching of the Word or moments of ministry that He came, but through personal, breathtaking visitations. Night after night, the presence of Jesus settled over the dormitories.

Many awoke with their eyes wide with wonder, saying, "Jesus visited me and showed me these things—what does it mean?" Some had seen themselves preaching before cameras, proclaiming the gospel across the Arab world. Others saw themselves shepherding churches not yet born. Still others saw faces, cities, and nations they would one day reach with the message of Christ's love.

It was breathtaking. God was revealing the end from the beginning—showing them that this was not just a school, but a place where He unveiled their purpose and destiny. Each dream, each vision, was an imprint of what the Lord had in store.

This was never about accumulating knowledge alone; it was about awakening identity. Every encounter was an invitation to walk in divine purpose and to know the depth of the Father's love. The Spirit was teaching what no book could contain, revealing God's plans deep in their hearts. Glory to God—how our hearts burned as we heard their reports in the mornings!

Heaven had its own curriculum, far beyond anything we could plan or teach on paper. God Himself was preparing these young men for lives of purpose we could hardly imagine. And I had the privilege—a privilege I will never take lightly—of witnessing it unfold right before my eyes.

When Prayer Crossed Borders

During one of our training sessions at the Centre, I sat at a plain wooden table on a balcony overlooking the tall cypress trees that lined the mountainside. The breeze carried their distinctive Cyprus scent—earthy, sharp, calming all at once. Six young men sat with me—men who, only months earlier, had been from the Arabic world. Now they were new creations in Christ—born again, filled with the Spirit, their faces glowing with a fire that still moves me to this day.

We began to worship with a simple chorus: "Alleluia."

The melody rose and fell like one shared breath—unpolished, unrehearsed, yet utterly pure. As we sang, the air thickened with Presence. The Holy Spirit descended—softly at first, then resting on us with a deep, tangible weight.

Then, suddenly, something shifted. The atmosphere changed. A holy stillness filled that balcony. There was no mistaking it: the Lord was in the place. And in that silence,

His clear word came, speaking straight to my heart: "There is a young man here who is concerned for a family member who is unwell back in his home country."

I breathed a quiet prayer under my breath. "Lord, who is it?"

And just as quickly as I asked, the Spirit answered. A name came clear and unmistakable: *Farid.* I lifted my eyes and looked across the table, steadying my voice though my heart was already stirring.

"Is there someone here burdened for a sick relative back home?" I asked gently.

The room grew quiet. Then I noticed tears forming in Farid's eyes. Slowly, almost hesitantly, he lifted his hand. When he spoke, his voice was soft yet heavy with grief and worry.

"Yes... my sister," he whispered. "She has a severe curvature in her spine. Her pain is unbearable. She is in the hospital in Amman. And... her husband wants to divorce her because she has not given him a son. In our culture, this brings shame. I think of her every day. It is hard to focus."

His words pierced my heart. It wasn't just his voice I heard—it was his anguish, unguarded and raw, spilling into the room. I could feel the depth of his love for his sister, the weight of shame pressing upon his family because she had not borne a son.

"Farid, if God has revealed this, then be assured—He

is both willing and able to heal her. Hold on to this truth: there is no distance in the Spirit. Even now, our prayers can reach her. Let's believe together."

So we joined hands around that simple wooden table, and with one heart and one voice, we sent the Word of God into that hospital room in Jordan. We commanded her spine to straighten, pain to leave, and healing to come in the mighty Name of Jesus.

After our time of prayer, we went downstairs for lunch. The room buzzed with the usual chatter as plates were passed, and laughter filled the air. Yet as I looked around the table, something struck me—Farid wasn't there. That was unusual. He always enjoyed mealtime.

When the meal ended, the students and I wandered out into the old sanatorium's front yard. The afternoon sun rested gently on the hills, casting a golden glow. Then, to my surprise, I saw a figure in the distance running up the hill toward us. Farid. His face was lit with pure joy, bursting with excitement he could hardly contain. I cupped my hands and called out, half laughing, half curious, "Farid! Where have you been? What's going on?"

Breathless but grinning, he reached the top of the hill. "I've been down at the bottom to make a phone call," he managed between breaths. "I called Jordan to check on my sister in the hospital to see what the Lord would do."

I was taken aback. His faith wasn't just lip service—it was action. He had believed so strongly that God had done something when we prayed that he went to find out by calling to see what had happened! "Tell me," I said, taking a breath. "What happened? What's the news?"

"You won't believe it! When I called, a nurse answered. She was so excited she could hardly get the words out. She kept saying, in Arabic, 'Your sister...your sister...your sister has been healed! She's healed! She's healed! Something has happened to her!'"

I stood there, stunned, hanging on every word as he continued. "The nurse said, 'Here is your sister, let her tell you herself,' and handed the phone to my sister. And then—" his voice broke with emotion. "And then my sister picked up the line. She was shouting, crying, screaming with joy, 'Farid! Farid, I have been healed! I'm healed! I'm healed!'"

As he was recounting the story, I could almost hear the commotion in that hospital room—the nurses rushing about, both bewildered and overjoyed. Farid had asked what had happened, and the answer shocked me.

"Around noon, a bright light came suddenly into her room, and out of nowhere, a wind like a tornado began to swirl and wrap itself around her body. The pain felt like it was being sucked right out of her. Then, suddenly, she heard popping sounds—pop, pop, pop—and instantly, all the pain was gone! She has no more pain! She's healed!"

Tears filled my eyes. I knew that the God we had called on in that quiet room had answered with power, stretching

His hand across borders. He had broken in and touched a girl in a hospital bed in Jordan at the very hour we prayed. Standing there on the hillside outside the sanatorium, I felt the awe of God's nearness, the sweetness of His presence.

And yet, the story wasn't finished. A number of months later, Farid came to me again, his face glowing with joy. His sister—the one who had been healed—was now pregnant. Even more, she was expecting a boy.

The husband who had been ready to cast her aside, shamed that she had not given him a son, was transformed. Instead of divorce, there was restoration. Their marriage was healed. The home, once overshadowed by sorrow, now rang with laughter, joy, and fresh beginnings.

They were blessed beyond measure by the Lord's goodness. Yet this was more than a healing—it was a demonstration of Christ's redemption. God had touched not only a broken body, but an entire household, rewriting their story in His great mercy and grace.

In the end, it was clear: when Jesus steps into brokenness, He never restores halfway. He restores fully, abundantly, and for His glory.

> *"I will restore to you the years that the swarming locust has eaten..." (Joel 2:25)*

What happened on that mountain in Cyprus was so much more than a single healing. It was a declaration from

Heaven—a sign that the breath of God had visited that place and was beginning to release life into everything it touched.

No border can stop the presence of God. No distance can silence His voice. No culture, no sickness, no shame, no circumstance lies beyond His reach.

In one moment of surrendered worship, the wind of Heaven swept from that mountain balcony into a distant hospital room, and God moved. He stepped into a room we had never entered and touched a body we had never seen. He healed a woman we had never met and restored an entire family we had only carried in prayer.

Farid's sister didn't just receive healing—she received a future. A marriage redeemed. A son promised. A destiny rewritten by the very hand of God. And those six young men—once bound by fear, religion, and darkness—saw with their own eyes that the Jesus who called them was not confined to their classroom, their mountain, or their nation.

I knew that the Spirit who moved here would move again. And again. And again.

Because wherever faith rises, hearts surrender, and people dare to believe that God still speaks and still acts, miracles become the language of everyday life.

That mountain on the island of Cyprus was never just a training ground. It was an altar. A furnace. A place kissed by the very presence of God—a witness to a gospel still alive, still burning, still breaking through the darkest places with unstoppable light.

Looking back, I could see it clearly. God had been moving me all along—step by step, nation by nation—preparing me for a work far greater than I could have imagined. From the dust of the Middle East to the snow of Scandinavia and into the fire of the island training centre, His hand had ordered every step. What once felt like uncertainty was, in truth, divine alignment unfolding in real time.

This chapter was never about geography.

It was about obedience—learning to trust the God who sees the end from the beginning, who knows precisely when to move us, where to send us, and how to prepare us for what lies ahead.

Each place carried its own refining, its own lesson in surrender—shaping my heart for what was still to come.

I did not choose this path. Heaven did.

I simply said yes.

And my friend, that same invitation stands before you.

God is still calling—patiently and lovingly—preparing hearts willing to trust Him beyond comfort and certainty.

He does not require perfection, only surrender.

Your yes can begin exactly where you are.

When you respond, the fire does not consume—it refines.

And for those who choose to follow, the journey is only beginning.

CHAPTER 9

A Voice That Cannot Be Silenced

Among the group of hungry young men in Cyprus was a student named Nabil—one of the remarkable young believers God had brought to our Bible school. His journey began as the son of a devout religious family. His childhood was steeped in a deeply traditional Middle Eastern faith background; he memorized the Quran from an early age and was expected to follow in his father's footsteps.

But God had other plans. Nabil first heard the gospel through a Christian radio program back in his home country. At first, he was angry. He wrote strong, impassioned letters to the broadcasters, determined to silence them with arguments.

But love and truth always have a way of breaking through. Over the years of correspondence, his heart softened. The walls of resistance fell, and one day, Nabil gave his life to Christ.

That decision cost him everything. When his family discovered his faith, they reacted with deep opposition, and he was forced from his home. As a teenager, he wandered homeless, abandoned by those he loved most. Yet even in the darkest nights, God never left him. Through divine connections, Nabil was brought to Cyprus—to the very Bible school where I was serving.

There, surrounded by other young believers who had come to Christ from similar backgrounds, his faith took root.

Earnest and enthusiastic, he longed to know Jesus more deeply. But when I taught on the baptism of the Holy Spirit, he resisted.

And the resistance continued for weeks. He sat through every class, polite but distant—his arms folded, his mind analysing every word. His church background from his Middle Eastern country had not prepared him for this kind of teaching on the Holy Spirit.

To him, the idea of being filled with the Spirit and speaking in tongues was unfamiliar—almost uncomfortable.

Yet even as he wrestled, I could sense the gentle pursuit

of God around him, the slow, steady pressure of grace softening a resistant heart. Then one night, close to midnight, there was a firm knock at my door.

I was preparing my lesson for the morning when I heard it—sharp, unexpected, insistent. When I opened the door, there stood Nabil—wide-eyed and visibly shaken up, his typical composure completely gone.

"Can I speak with you?" he asked, his voice low and unsteady.

"Of course," I said, stepping aside and inviting him in. He entered slowly, his hands slightly shaky. After a long pause, he looked at me and started to speak.

"I had a dream," he said, his tone already breaking. "A very real dream—like I was there." He stopped for a moment, gathering his words.

"I saw a great banquet table," he continued softly. "And on this large table were many bottles of wine. Jesus was at the center of the table. The director—the visionary—was on one side, and you, Anthony, were on the other. You both were laughing, full of joy, drinking freely from the bottles of wine, having as much as you desired. The room was filled with celebration.

"And then..." His voice faltered. "Then Jesus turned toward me. His eyes were full of love. And He said, 'Nabil, there's more if you want it.'" Nabil's eyes filled with tears. "Then I woke up."

As he spoke, the presence of God filled the room. I could feel it—thick, holy, unmistakable. Tears welled up in my eyes as I smiled.

"Nabil," I said softly, "Jesus is showing you that He has more for you—the fullness of His Spirit. Do you want it?"

His answer came like a cry from deep within his soul. "Yes! Yes, I want it!"

In that moment, Heaven opened. I placed my hands upon his head, and before I could even pray a full sentence, the power of the Holy Spirit fell, and it was sudden, overwhelming, and undeniable. Nabil began to tremble, then lifted his hands. A heavenly language poured from his mouth—fluent, beautiful, like rivers breaking through a dam.

Tears streamed down his face as the joy of the Lord filled him to overflowing. Minutes turned into hours. He prayed in tongues without ceasing, lost in worship, consumed by the reality of God's love. The room itself seemed to vibrate with His presence—alive, pure, and holy. When at last he could speak, his words came through laughter, tears, and amazement.

That night, everything changed. The skeptic became a believer. The student became a witness.

From that day forward, Nabil could not stop speaking about the Holy Spirit. His face shone with the same fire he once doubted. His prayers carried power, and his words carried life. Each time I saw him, I remembered—this is how great awakenings begin: one life set ablaze at a time, until whole nations catch the flame.

The Legacy Continues

Years later, I received an update on Nabil. He was no longer just a student in a hidden Bible school—he had become a preacher on satellite television, boldly proclaiming Christ to multitudes across the Arabic world. For more than 25 years now, his ministry has touched countless souls for the Kingdom of God.

However, significant opposition has followed him every step of the way. The threats against his life are real, and at times, he has been forced to minister discreetly.

Yet the fire that first fell on him during that midnight encounter in Cyprus has never gone out. He continues pressing forward with deep courage, carrying the gospel into places where traditional missionaries cannot go.

Today, Nabil hosts a powerful television program that reaches the broader Middle East. This broadcast features dynamic testimonies of believers from diverse faith backgrounds, giving them a platform to share what Christ has done in their lives.

The response has been overwhelming. Thousands of viewers have called the prayer line or visited the ministry's websites. Many have prayed to receive Jesus Christ as their Savior, right there in their living rooms, while listening to his voice.

Nabil's story is more than remarkable—it is a living testimony of what happens when the Holy Spirit takes hold of a surrendered life. From a homeless teenager cast out of his home to a voice reaching nations, his journey reminds us of this powerful truth: the Spirit doesn't just transform individuals; He raises them up to transform the world!

Here I Am, Lord

There are seasons when God prepares His greatest works—not in cathedrals or public arenas, but in secret places where hearts burn unseen. The "Hidden School" was never just a Bible training centre; it was the upper room of the Middle East, a place where Heaven quietly prepared voices that would one day shake nations.

What looked concealed to man was fully visible to the Lord. Behind closed doors and drawn curtains, the Spirit of God was igniting hearts once bound by fear, religion, and oppression. These were not mere students—they were living flames, men marked by encounter and willing to risk everything for the One who had rescued them. Heaven was writing a story in silence, and those whispers of obedience would become a roar of revival across nations.

There, unknown to man, God revealed one of His greatest truths: the call of God rarely begins in comfort; it begins in surrender. It was not prestige that drew them, but Presence. It was not curiosity, but covenant love—a love that overcomes fear, silences doubt, and compels one to go where angels tread softly.

When I heard His voice calling me to Cyprus—to stand alongside these heroes of faith—I realized something profound: God doesn't call the qualified; He qualifies the called. One yes to His whisper can set in motion a ripple that reaches eternity.

Every divine assignment begins as a seed—small, obscure, vulnerable—but within it lies a forest of destiny. These students, unknown to the world, became carriers of resurrection life. Their classroom was not only a place of learning but also a place of dying—dying to self, to safety, to reputation. Yet in that death, the life of Christ blossomed. They discovered that when you lose everything for Jesus, you gain the one thing that can never be taken from you: His presence.

Nabil's story reminds us that the gospel still burns brightest in the darkest places. That the Kingdom of God does not advance by might or by power, but by the Spirit of God. Even the smallest acts of obedience—no matter how seemingly insignificant, no matter how trembling—can shape generations to come.

Beloved, the same Holy Spirit that whispered to those students speaks softly to us now. You may never stand in a Middle Eastern classroom or on a global platform, but the One who calls has prepared you for a purpose. The hidden season is not a delay; it is divine preparation. In the silence, He is shaping your voice, refining your heart, and awakening your courage for the hour ahead.

If He can turn pain into testimony, persecution into power, and secrecy into a sound that shakes nations, then what can He do through a surrendered life like yours?

Dare to believe again. The same Spirit that raised Jesus from the dead dwells in you. The same God who raised up fiery witnesses in the Middle East is still searching for yielded hearts—people who will say, "Here am I, Lord, send me."

The Fire Still Burns

The "set-apart school" was never merely a training centre—it was a place of encounter. Behind closed doors and far from public view, God was shaping voices the world had yet to hear. He was taking the rejected and clothing them with radiance, taking the silenced and giving them a sound that would carry far beyond those walls.

Nabil was one of those vessels—a young man marked by loss, shaped by suffering, and then overtaken by the love of Jesus and the fire of the Holy Spirit. What began in resistance ended in surrender. What began with questions became a calling sealed by God Himself.

Years later, the same man who once argued against the gospel now proclaims it with boldness. The same life that once wandered homeless now carries hope into homes across the Middle East. And though persecution still shadows his steps, the fire ignited in that midnight encounter has never gone out. It continues to burn—steady, pure, and unashamed.

This is the legacy of the Holy Spirit. He turns hidden obedience into public fruit. He redeems what the enemy meant to destroy and fashions it into a testimony of grace and power. He lights torchbearers that cannot be silenced, because they were ignited by Heaven itself.

And that fire still burns.

Reflection: Your Surrender Can Rewrite a Generation

Let's take a moment, friend. Pause and let your heart grow quiet before the Lord.

You've just read about Nabil's journey—his surrender, his suffering, his obedience, and the supernatural call of God that turned one young man into a voice to the nations. But now I want to gently turn the question toward *you.*

What is the Holy Spirit stirring in your heart right now?

Not 10 years from now. Not when life becomes easier. But now—in this very moment.

Ask Him:

"Lord, what are You inviting me into?"

"What step of obedience are You whispering to my heart?"

"What fear do You want to break off of me?"

"Where are You calling me to say yes?"

Don't rush. Let His voice—not pressure, not guilt, not striving—speak softly to your spirit.

He may bring to mind a person, a place, a conversation, a dream you've buried, a gift you've hidden, a calling you've avoided, or simply a deeper surrender to His presence. Whatever rises in your heart, pay attention. Those whispers often carry the seeds of destiny.

I want you to ask Him one more question:

"Lord, what would You do through my life if I simply said yes?"

Sit with that for a moment and let it stretch your faith. Let it awaken something that's been asleep and stir the embers of hunger inside you.

And now hear this—prophetically, tenderly, personally: **God has not forgotten you.** You are not hidden by accident—you are hidden by design. The same God who visited Nabil in a dream, who whispered to young men on a mountain, who crossed borders to heal Farid's sister, who turned persecuted teenagers into fiery witnesses...is the God who is preparing you.

The seed He planted in you still carries power. The calling He whispered still carries weight. The yes you offer today may become the testimony that shakes someone else's world tomorrow.

Heaven is not looking for the impressive. Heaven is looking for the yielded. If you dare to believe and trust Him with your story, your life may become the flame that sets another heart on fire. A spark that lights a generation.

So let this be your prayer:

"Lord, here I am. I say yes. Speak, and I will obey. Lead, and I will follow. Use my life for Your glory, whether in hidden rooms or on global stages. My yes belongs to You."

Friend, this is how revival begins. Not with crowds, but with one surrendered heart. And Heaven is listening for yours.

CHAPTER 10

The Yes That Changed Everything

I didn't see it coming.

In 2004, I began feeling a strange stirring—an unshakable sense that God was preparing to move me to another nation. It didn't come with details or explanations; it came like a gentle tug on the heart, a whisper that wouldn't leave. Around that time, I stayed in touch with a beautiful Finnish family I had come to love during my years in Israel. Our paths had crossed through ministry, and a deep friendship had formed.

Then one day, without warning, an invitation crossed my inbox: "Anthony, would you come to Finland and preach revival meetings in our town?"

As I read their words, something leapt inside me. The

stirring I'd been feeling suddenly aligned, and the whisper became a direction. What began as a simple invitation quickly revealed itself as the next chapter God had been preparing all along.

Though excitement and anticipation immediately flooded my heart as I read their email, I knew I still had to wait on the Lord in prayer. After much seeking, He faithfully confirmed that it was indeed His will—He was sending me to Europe. He assured me that His presence would go with me and that He would open doors among the Finnish people.

And truly, He did.

In Finland, the Lord blessed our efforts beyond what we could have imagined. We held revival meetings lasting eight to ten weeks at a time, moving from town to town as the Spirit led. Each gathering carried a unique touch of Heaven—souls were saved, lives were healed, many were baptized in the Holy Spirit, and hearts were set ablaze for God. It was a glorious season in the Lord.

Oh, how I came to love the beautiful people of Finland—their sincerity, their warmth, and their quiet strength. What an amazing nation, full of lakes and long summer nights, where the northern lights dance across the sky, and fellowship is often shared over hot saunas, fresh *pulla*, and strong coffee!

So It Began

After a year of traveling across Finland in ministry, the Holy Spirit spoke clearly to my heart. His voice was unmistakable—gentle, yet filled with authority: He wanted me to plant my first church on the southern border of Finland, just across from Russia.

At first, I wrestled with the call. My heart was stirred, yet my mind resisted. "Lord," I reasoned, "I'm an evangelist, not a pastor. Are You sure You want me to start a church? That would mean stepping into something completely new—a shift from preaching revival to shepherding hearts."

He didn't answer with words, but His presence spoke louder than any sentence ever could. The conviction within me grew stronger by the day. I could feel His hand guiding me, His Spirit whispering, *"Trust Me, and follow."*

The desire to establish a gathering—a home for His presence, a place where His glory could dwell—quickly started burning deep within my soul.

And so, with a small group of passionate believers, including a young man from Norway, several devoted families, and a handful of young people hungry for God, we began to pioneer what would become a Spirit-filled church. It was humble in its beginnings—no grand building, no fanfare—just a handful of hearts united by one cry: "Come, Holy Spirit."

And it was a cry that Heaven heard.

The fire of God began to spread, and the meetings were marked by a tangible sense of His presence. At times, the atmosphere grew so thick with His glory that words became unnecessary—only tears, worship, and awe remained.

For the next 10 years, I had the privilege of pastoring that congregation, watching the Holy Spirit move mightily among us. One of the young men who was introduced to me during that season became a dear spiritual son. He had been a heroin addict, bound by darkness and despair. But through the mercy of God—and the faithful prayers of his family and his good aunt—our paths crossed. Over time, I watched the Lord's hand move powerfully in his life. He was completely healed, delivered, and transformed into a radical lover and follower of Jesus Christ.

Today, he and his beautiful wife oversee a thriving church in Finland, where they live and serve the Lord faithfully. The grace of God upon their lives is nothing short of remarkable—a shining testimony of redemption that continues to inspire me to this day. He is just one of many young people whose lives were forever transformed by the power of God during that unforgettable season of revival in Finland.

A Mighty Outpouring in Russia

During those 10 remarkable years in Finland, God began opening doors I never could have imagined. Opportunities seemed to unfold one after another—unexpected, unplanned, yet unmistakably divine. One of those doors led to Russia. I received an invitation to minister in local Russian churches, and then, in a completely surprising turn, to preach inside a drug and rehabilitation centre in Saint Petersburg.

What began as a simple step of obedience was becoming a doorway into lives marked by brokenness, addiction, and deep spiritual hunger.

When the opportunity came, our church was overjoyed. We sensed it was a divine assignment. Together, we prepared for a short-term mission trip, gathering a team of passionate young believers eager to serve. Our purpose was simple yet powerful—to spend several days ministering to men and women who had been delivered from addiction and tell them that the same Jesus who saves also heals, restores, and gives new life.

The man leading the charge was no ordinary director. He was a man of God who had received a divine vision and deep compassion from the Lord to rescue those the world had forgotten. Out of that vision, this rehabilitation centre was born—a place where broken lives were restored and the light of Christ reached into the darkest corners of human suffering.

When we arrived, the rehabilitation director greeted me and began to share the story of their work. At that time, there were about 150 former heroin users living in the facility. Many had been rescued from the underground sewer systems of Saint Petersburg—places where they had once shot up and been left for dead.

I was deeply moved as he continued to share. A few minutes later, to my surprise, he paused in the middle of his story and looked me deep in the eyes. "Anthony, thank you so much for coming," he began kindly. "But I want you to know—it's been hard going here, especially when it comes to seeing these former addicts truly come to salvation. Over the past year and a half, only a handful have been born again. It would probably be best not to get your expectations too high. We've been preaching to this group for quite some time, and only a small number have responded to Christ. The rest...well, they haven't. So, please, don't expect too much."

His words hit me like a ton of bricks. This was *not* the kind of encouragement I was expecting! To be honest, my first thought was, "*You mean I've come all the way to Saint Petersburg in faith—having prayed, prepared, and paid the cost—believing God for great things, only to be told not to hope for too much? To not expect people to respond to the gospel message?*"

Now, don't misunderstand me. I had deep respect for this man of God. He had sacrificed so much, literally pouring out his life for these former addicts. Still, his words were hard to swallow. Everything in me wanted to believe that God could do far more than what we ask, think, or imagine (Ephesians 3:20). Deep down, I knew the Lord hadn't brought me all this way just to witness a few salvations. He had something far greater in mind.

I'm not even sure what I said—something like, "Well, I believe God can still do the impossible." With that, I smiled, thanked him, and quietly walked away, my heart whispering a very different expectation. As I stepped outside, I couldn't shake the feeling—I just couldn't agree with that statement. How could I, when I knew deep in my heart that with God, all things are possible?

I decided to take a short walk and found myself beside a nearby brown-coloured river flowing quietly behind the centre. There, with the cool air brushing past and the steady rhythm of the water beside me, I began to pray.

"Lord," I said, "this doesn't feel right. You've placed expectation in my heart—not for small things, but for great things. I believe You want to save, heal, and deliver these precious people." As I prayed, a question rose in my spirit: if I were one of these addicts hearing the gospel for the very first time—and this might be my only chance to hear it—how would I want it preached?

The answer came quickly and clearly: *"I'd want it preached loud, strong, full of fire, and very clear!"*

Right then and there, I made a quiet resolve before God: when the time came, I would hold nothing back—I would give them everything I had.

The Gospel Proclaimed

Finally, the moment came. Over 150 former drug addicts filled the room, their faces marked with stories of pain, yet their eyes flickering with hope. I opened Luke 4:18 and began to proclaim the words that burned in my spirit:

The Spirit of the Lord is upon Me,
because He has anointed Me
to preach the gospel to the poor;
He has sent Me to heal the brokenhearted,
to proclaim liberty to the captives
and recovery of sight to the blind,
to set at liberty those who are oppressed.

Each phrase exploded from my heart. I preached with conviction—that if Jesus did it then, He would surely do it now. It felt like a freight train roaring through a small town. The word was unstoppable, alive, filled with divine urgency. My interpreter could hardly keep up as I poured out the message with everything in me.

When I finished, I knew it was time to release faith for salvation. My heart pounded as I lifted my eyes to the crowd. "Who here wants to give their heart to Jesus Christ?" I asked.

For a moment, the room was still. Then, one hand went up—then another—and another. Within seconds, it was as if a wave swept through the crowd. Hands were raised everywhere. I would estimate that at least 98 percent wanted to receive Christ.

I glanced toward the director, whose eyes were wide with disbelief and awe. The altar was flooded with people. They prayed the prayer of salvation with passion, tears streaming, voices roaring in surrender. As I walked among them, laying hands and praying, I saw faces frail from years of pain and addiction. My heart broke. Then one young woman stepped forward, her voice trembling: "You preached that Jesus not only saves, but also heals. Please pray that God will heal my AIDS. I believe He can heal me."

Her words pierced me. Later, I learned that nearly 85 percent of those in the center had AIDS. And now I stood before them—about to lay hands on 145 or so AIDS patients. My faith was tested to the core. But the Word of God burned within me. I had just preached that Jesus saves, heals, and delivers. How could I do anything but stand on that truth?

So I stood.

And I believed.

One by one, I laid my hands upon them all, praying the prayer of faith over each precious life. "By His stripes we are healed," I declared again and again. By the time I reached the last person, the atmosphere was electric, thick with God's presence. Heaven had drawn near. It was a mighty move of the Holy Spirit—one I will never forget.

When the final "amen" was spoken, we lifted our hands and rejoiced together, giving thanks for all that the Lord had done. Not long after, our team returned to Finland humbled, grateful, and still in awe of the God who saves and heals.

A Return Visit

Three months later, I was invited back to Saint Petersburg. When I walked once again through the doors of that rehabilitation center, I had no idea that the Lord had already written a continuation to the story.

As I entered the main hall, a young woman came running toward me—her face radiant, her smile wide and full of light. "Pastor Anthony! Pastor Anthony! Do you remember me?" she exclaimed, her voice trembling with excitement.

I hesitated, searching her face. "I'm sorry...remind me. Who are you?"

Her laughter overflowed. "I was at your meeting a few months ago! I had never heard about the gospel, and I gave my heart to Jesus that night—and I've had so much peace and joy ever since!"

I smiled, moved by her passion. "That's wonderful," I said quietly, giving thanks.

But she wasn't finished. "That's not all," she continued, her eyes sparkling. "I was also baptized in the Holy Spirit, and I speak in tongues—just like you preached! Praise the Lord!"

I laughed with joy. "That's amazing! Glory to God!"

Then her tone shifted, her eyes softening. "But, Pastor Anthony...that's still not all." Tears welled as she spoke, her voice cracking. "I had AIDS for four years because of my drug use. That night, when you preached that Jesus heals, I came forward for prayer. A week later, I began to feel stronger—different. I knew something had changed. So I asked the director if I could go to Saint Petersburg for blood tests."

The director was hesitant, fearing she might relapse back to drugs again. But she persisted for days until he finally agreed she could go.

She continued, her eyes sparkling bright, "Pastor Anthony, I took four blood tests. Every single one came back the same. They could not find a trace of AIDS in my body. The doctors said it was impossible—but I told them, 'It's a miracle. Jesus healed me!'"

Her words filled the air, and for a long moment, silence fell. Then joy erupted. There are no words to describe the light that filled that moment—the awe, the gratitude, the holy witness and presence of God that we felt.

Jesus Christ had once again revealed Himself as the same yesterday, today, and forever. He had healed her completely. He had proven that His compassion still reaches into the lowest places to lift the broken and restore what the world has declared impossible.

Tears of thanksgiving streamed down my face as I whispered, "Jesus never changes—not for one moment. He is, and always will be, the same. Praise the Lord—great things He has done!"

Standing there in that rehabilitation centre in Saint Petersburg, a deep realization settled in my heart—one I would never forget. Everything that had unfolded in that moment had hinged on a single yes.

A yes to leave Israel.

A yes to go to Finland.

A yes to plant a church.

A yes to cross borders.

A yes to preach with expectation when others had lost it.

Each step began the same way—with a simple yes.

And now, the invitation extends beyond my story.

Jesus is still waiting—waiting for your yes, just as He continues to wait for mine. Not a perfect yes. Not a fully mapped-out yes. Just a willing one. A surrendered one.

When we say yes to Him, our lives do not remain the same. Paths shift. Hearts awaken. Ordinary moments become holy ground. What begins as a quiet response often unfolds into an adventure we never could have planned—yet one we would never trade.

This book is not merely the record of where I have been. It is an invitation into where He longs to take you.

So wherever you find yourself—at the beginning, in the middle, or standing on the edge of something unknown—

pause and listen. Hear His gentle call. Trust His faithfulness. Offer Him your yes.

Because one surrendered yes can open heaven, rewrite destinies, and change everything.

And He is still saying,

"Follow Me."

A Prayer for Miracles

My friend, I believe in miracles because I simply believe in God. I want you to know that what may seem impossible to men is indeed possible because we still serve the God of miracles.

A miracle, by its very nature, is something you cannot comprehend or explain. If you can understand it, then it is not a miracle. God wants to amaze you with His loving awe and His wonder in your life right now. I sense the gift of impartation—a grace to receive a miracle—through your personal faith reaching out to Jesus.

But first, we must remember this beautiful truth: He heals us because He loves us. It really is that simple.

Father, right now, we take this moment and come into Your presence by the blood of the Lamb.

Lord, we decree and declare that Your finished work is an accomplished work—fully available to all who put their trust in You. Through the power of the Holy Spirit, in the name of Jesus Christ, I release the anointing of the

Lord to heal, to mend, to restore every place that hurts, and to make a way where there seems to be no way.

Lord God, we thank You for the power of Your Spirit penetrating every cell, every muscle tissue, every organ, and every circumstance of Your precious reader. Holy Spirit, let Your anointing touch them. Let them receive Your healing grace and Your provision.

Lord, thank You for what You are doing even now, both seen and unseen. For the miracle already in motion, and for Your tender love and care.

Amen.

Right now, you may begin sense the warmth of the Holy Spirit—His surrounding presence, His mighty power resting upon your life.

The presence of Jesus Christ is touching your heart, your soul, and your physical body, doing what only He can do. He is bringing healing and restoration.

Acknowledge His touch and thank Him for His presence. Recognize the deep and beautiful work He is doing in your life today.

In Jesus' name, I declare and decree: **you will never be the same.**

Father God, we give You glory.
Lord Jesus, we give You praise.
Holy Spirit, thank You for Your mighty touch.
We receive the miracle. In Jesus' name. Amen.

CHAPTER 11

Resurrection Life, Way Down Under

In 2004, while living in Finland, I set aside time to seek the Lord for the year ahead. Winters there are long and still—snow lying heavy across the streets, the silence becoming a sanctuary where prayer feels near enough to touch.

One evening, clear as a bell, I heard it in my spirit: "Australia."

The word startled me. *Australia?* It had never once crossed my mind. It wasn't a place I'd ever dreamed of visiting or even thought much about. To be honest, I'd never had the slightest desire to see a kangaroo—much less go halfway around the world to find one. The thought felt completely out of the blue. It was so unexpected, so far from anything familiar I would have ever imagined.

As I searched my memory, wondering if there was anyone I might possibly know there, one person came to mind—a kind lady who had once visited our church in Finland. She lived in Tasmania, a small island tucked away at the very edge of the world, a place I could barely locate on a map. Yet somehow, that tiny name on the globe began to stir something deep inside me.

The more I prayed, the stronger it grew. It wasn't just a passing thought; I couldn't shake it. It felt as though Heaven itself was charting a course I couldn't yet see—drawing me toward something unknown, something divine, something waiting just beyond the horizon.

It was one of those moments you simply cannot ignore. God had spoken. And when He speaks, there is only one response—obedience. I remember sitting quietly, letting the weight of it settle in my spirit. There was no thunder, no flash of lightning—just that unmistakable certainty that comes when God has made His will known. The word Australia echoed again and again in my heart, until it became impossible to dismiss.

At that time, Annette and I were newly married, just beginning our life together. Everything felt fresh—our faith, our marriage, our dreams for the future. And yet, this call from God was unlike anything we had ever imagined. It meant leaving behind what was familiar—our friends, our routines, even the comfort of the life we were just starting to build.

But deep down, we both knew that when God calls, you go.

So, after much prayer and seeking the Lord's peace, we made the decision—together and with expectant faith—that we would go to Australia. We didn't have every detail worked out. We didn't know what awaited us on the other side of the world. But we knew who had spoken. And that was enough.

The day we boarded the plane, my heart pounded with a mix of excitement and holy anticipation. Everything familiar was behind us; everything unknown lay just ahead. It felt like stepping onto a blank page in God's story—waiting for Him to write the next chapter.

When we finally landed in Tasmania, it was as though we had stepped into another world. Mist-crowned mountains rose over rolling green hills, their peaks hidden in clouds like mysteries waiting to be revealed. Dense forests stretched like oceans of trees. Rivers glistened in the sunlight, winding softly through the land. Along the coast, waves rolled against the cliffs, and beaches shone with a warm, golden glow.

Everywhere, creation declared the glory of God.

Tasmania didn't just impress the eye—it touched the soul. The air felt fresh and full of life. The quiet carried a peaceful stillness, as if the land itself was waiting for the

Spirit to move. Deep inside, I knew. This was not just a move. This was a divine assignment.

And here, in this land of wilderness and wonder, God began to write new adventures—miracles and encounters that would shape our lives forever.

Sixty-Seven Minutes to Resurrection

After a few years of living in Tasmania, my wife's parents flew in from England, overflowing with excitement to experience Australia for the very first time. Everything felt new and alive to them: the endless blue skies, the scent of eucalyptus drifting through the air, the strange and beautiful birds they had never heard before. Even the sunlight seemed different—a brightness that felt both gentle and vivid at the same time. Their joy was contagious; their wonder, pure and childlike.

That morning, with excitement that could not be contained, they made one simple request: "We want to see kangaroos!" It was such an innocent desire—one of those simple dreams that make a journey unforgettable. So, we drove them to the local zoo. My wife and I had been there many times before, so we decided to let them enjoy the experience on their own. Their faces lit up as we dropped them off—they could hardly wait to see the sights!

After waving goodbye, we headed back toward town. My wife asked to stop at a nearby fast-food shop. She went inside, and I stayed in the car. Everything felt normal—just another errand, another quiet moment. I had no idea how quickly the ordinary was about to turn into the extraordinary. Within minutes, I would be thrust into one of the most unforgettable and life-changing moments of my life and ministry.

Suddenly, through the hum of traffic, I heard a desperate cry. "Someone help me! My mate is dead! My mate is dead!" Without thinking, I flung open the car door and ran across the road.

A frantic man was shouting for help, struggling to pull his friend from the backseat of a car that had screeched to a stop. I rushed to his side, and together we managed to lift the man out, laying his motionless body on the roadside.

In that instant, time seemed to slow. The sound of traffic faded, and all I could hear was the pounding of my own heartbeat. The man's skin and lips were already turning blue. His body was stiff, heavy, lifeless.

He wasn't breathing. He was gone.

A sweep of adrenaline ran through me—not from fear, but from the sheer weight of the moment. I knew I was standing in a place where life and eternity were about to meet.

We were out in the rural outskirts, nearly 45 minutes from town—hardly the place you'd want to be in a medical emergency. An ambulance could take quite a long time, and time was the one thing this man didn't have.

I dropped to my knees beside him, slipping my hands

beneath his shoulders to steady his lifeless body. His friend was already bent over him, frantic and undone—tears streaming as he tried desperately to force life back into him. He breathed into his mouth, then pressed down hard against his chest with trembling hands, counting, sobbing, pleading all at once.

"Oh my goodness—he has a wife and family! He has children! What am I going to do?" he cried, his voice breaking in despair.

I held the man steady and began to pray, quietly at first, but with growing urgency. My lips barely moved, yet inside my spirit, the cry was fierce. Time seemed to stretch; every second felt like an eternity. Ten minutes...twenty...nearly thirty...and still, there was no sign of life.

A small crowd began to gather, their faces fixed on the heart-stopping, real-life moment. The only sounds were the desperate gasps of the man's friend and the steady rhythm of the compressions he kept giving.

Finally, after what felt like an eternity, the paramedics finally arrived. They moved quickly—professional, composed, and focused. Within moments, the defibrillator was ready.

"Clear!" one of them shouted. The paddles pressed down.

Once.

Twice.

Three times.

Still nothing.

After 67 minutes without a heartbeat, the lead paramedic finally spoke the words that hung heavy in the air: "He's gone."

The man was pronounced dead. The air hung thick with silence, the kind that follows final words no one wants to hear.

But deep within me, a still, unwavering conviction of faith surged up inside—a faith that only God could give. It was stronger than fear, louder than doubt. And I was about to touch Heaven at the throne of God.

He was not finished.

My wife joined shortly after, and we both stepped back from the growing crowd and found a small rise overlooking the roadside scene. From that vantage point, we could see everything—the cluster of bystanders pressing in, the flashing lights in the distance, the friend still kneeling beside the motionless body. Still, my faith continued stirring—steady, insistent, unrelenting.

I looked toward Heaven and lifted my voice in prayer.

> *"Lord, this man has most likely split hell wide open, not knowing you. But You are the Resurrection and the Life. In the mighty name of Jesus, I command his spirit to come back to his body. Give him another chance, Father—not only to be healed, but to know You. In Jesus' Name I pray. Annette and I agree."*

As the words left my lips, a deep assurance filled me—an unshakable peace that can only come from the presence of God. Fear and doubt had come and gone.

Immediately after praying, the Lord gave me a vision so real, it felt as though I were there. I saw the man alive again, sitting upright in a hospital bed, smiling with quiet joy as he ate yogurt from a small cup. His family stood around him in the shape of a horseshoe, their eyes wide with awe and hearts flooded with peace and relief.

And in that moment, standing on that small hill above the chaos, I knew—Heaven had heard. Faith had spoken. And God was about to move.

I turned to Annette, my wife, and said, "It's done. Let's not look back. Let's go to the car and thank God for what He's done." We agreed.

Suddenly, a surge of shouting erupted from the crowd. The ambulance drivers who had been standing over the lifeless body were now yelling—voices cracking with shock and triumph.

"He's alive! He's alive! Oh my God—he's alive!"

There was an instant eruption of gasps, screams, and tears as the paramedics sprang into action. They lifted his body—*the same man who had shown no heartbeat for well over an hour*—and quickly placed him into the ambulance. The sirens wailed as they rushed him toward the Royal Hobart Hospital.

Annette and I stood there, stunned and overwhelmed by the awesome presence of God. A holy stillness wrapped around us as the crowd continued to buzz with disbelief and joy.

We could hardly process what we were witnessing: a man—dead for what seemed like an eternity—was now alive.

They kept shouting it over and over as the ambulance doors slammed shut:

"He made it! He made it! He's alive!"

The excitement was electric. We had just watched God do the impossible, and this moment would mark us forever.

The Third-Day Awakening

The next day, we had no natural knowledge of the man's condition. The last time we had seen him was when the paramedics drove him away. Still, we couldn't shake the burden to pray. We began reaching out to close friends and local churches, asking them to intercede for his full recovery.

Word spread quickly. Soon, churches across the region were lifting their voices in prayer, crying out for the man's healing. Faith was alive in Tasmania—palpable, rising like incense before the throne of God.

As the story progressed, it was on the third day when,

in the middle of my daily routine, I suddenly heard the Holy Spirit gently whisper, "I want you to call the hospital and see what I have done."

Did I hear that right? Lord, is that really You? I wondered. But I knew in my spirit—it was Him.

So, with trepidation, I picked up the phone and called the hospital to inquire about the man and his condition. When the nurse answered the phone, her tone was professional and calm.

I took a deep breath and went straight into it. "I would like to know how the man who was taken in yesterday from the countryside where the incident occurred is doing," I said, giving her his name.

She replied, "Are you a relative?"

"No," I answered discreetly, "but I was there when he collapsed, helping in the resuscitation process, and I would really like to know, please."

Silence.

The line went quiet, stretching longer than I could bear. My stomach tightened. For a brief moment, doubt crept in. Had I misunderstood? Had the man slipped away after all?

Then, at last, the nurse spoke again. Her words came slowly, carefully—each one deliberate, though she was still trying to believe them herself. "He's no longer in intensive care..."

Another pause. My breath caught in my throat.

Then she continued, her voice softer but even steadier:

"He's been moved out of intensive care and into a private room. He's doing well, and his family is with him, celebrating. Not only that, but he's even gone to the toilet on his own several times today."

I froze, unable to speak. My mind struggled to process what I had just heard.

Sixty-seven minutes without a heartbeat—yet now a man restored. Walking. Talking. A living proof that Jesus Christ is the Resurrection and the Life. The God who raised Lazarus had done it again. And as the reality settled over me, one truth thundered through my spirit:

This is the Jesus we serve: the One who steps into impossible moments, the One who rewrites death with life, the One who still moves in raw, undeniable power.

This miracle didn't just touch one man—it shook a city. It changed everything.

Conclusion: A Final Invitation

Standing there in Tasmania, at what felt like the far edge of the world, a quiet truth settled in my heart: resurrection life knows no geography. It is not confined to holy cities or moments we label as extraordinary. The same power that raised Jesus from the dead was present there, too—near, gentle, and alive.

As I reflected on the journey, from the cold winters of Finland to the sunlit roads of Australia, I saw a consistent thread woven through it all. Jesus had been faithful every step of the way. His nature had never changed—only the landscape. And even in places far removed from where the story began, His voice still carried authority, and life still responded.

That moment in Tasmania was not just about a miracle. It felt like an invitation to pause and notice something deeper: the risen Christ continues to meet us in ordinary moments, often quietly and unexpectedly. Sometimes all it takes is a simple prayer, a small step of obedience, or a yes offered without certainty—and Heaven gently moves in response.

Across nations and seasons, His resurrection life continues to reach, restore, and awaken hearts. Often unseen, but always intentional.

Everything I have witnessed—every healing, every life changed—has flowed not from striving or effort, but from relationship. From learning to walk with the Holy Spirit as a Person: present, faithful, and kind. He has always led me back to Jesus. He has always glorified the Son. And in quiet ways, He has brought Heaven into everyday life.

And this is why I can say, simply and sincerely: **I love You, Holy Spirit.**

What I have learned over time is this: when Jesus is welcomed, the Holy Spirit is free to work. And when the Holy Spirit is welcomed, lives are never the same!

The same Spirit who was present at the empty tomb now dwells within every believer. He is not distant. He is not selective. He is not limited to certain places or people. You can know Him too. You can learn to walk with Him, become familiar with His voice, and live a life shaped by His presence.

These stories are not shared to impress, but to invite. The same Jesus who has met people across nations and cultures is quietly inviting you closer—not with pressure, but with love.

God has always worked through ordinary people who are willing to trust Him one step at a time. Many of the most meaningful stories are never told—lives marked by faithfulness, unseen obedience, and prayers whispered in hope.

Heaven sees those lives.

And you can be one of them.

So as you close this book, I offer a gentle invitation:

Draw nearer to Jesus.

Open your heart to the Holy Spirit.

Pay attention to the quiet nudges.

Be willing to say yes, even in small ways.

And trust this: if resurrection life can be revealed in Tasmania, it can be revealed anywhere—and in anyone—who believes that Jesus Christ is still the Resurrection and the Life.

A FINAL PRAYER FOR THE READER

Receiving His Presence, Grace, and Power

Father God, in the precious name of Jesus Christ, I thank You for Jesus—for all that we have received, and all that we will ever receive, comes first and fully through Him.

And yet, Lord, it is through the indwelling, empowering presence of the Holy Spirit that this immeasurable gift is made real to us—the gift of the Holy Spirit Himself, freely given to all who place their trust in You.

And now, in Jesus' name, we welcome the presence and power of the Holy Spirit—the One who overshadowed Mary, the One who raised Jesus from the dead, and the One who empowered the early disciples to proclaim the gospel and bear witness that Christ is truly alive.

Holy Spirit, we love You.

We honour and welcome You.

We invite You here among us, even now.

I release, in the mighty name of Jesus, the blessing and resurrection life of Christ over every reader whose heart is hungry and whose spirit longs for more of You.

Holy Spirit, come—quicken hearts and awaken faith. Touch deeply. Heal gently. Minister personally. Let Your empowering presence rest upon each life today.

Father, thank You for the impartation of Your grace, Your love, and Your mercy.

Thank You for Your gifts, freely given—and above all, for Your beloved presence, which brings wholeness, renewal, and peace, and draws us into deeper intimacy with You.

From this moment forward, may every reader know the sweet fellowship of the Holy Spirit— learning to yield to Him, to recognise His voice, and to walk in step with His gentle leading.

And as they do, may the life and power of Christ flow through them—to love faithfully,

to serve humbly, and to reflect the heart of Jesus wherever they go.

And like the disciples of old, may it be said of them that they, too, had the privilege of seeing this world turned upside down for Jesus Christ.

Holy Spirit, we love You. Have Your way.

Acknowledgments

I want to first express my deepest gratitude to my amazing wife, **Annette**, who has walked faithfully by my side through every season of this journey. Your steadfast love, patience, and unwavering faith have continually strengthened me. You have spoken life into me when I was weary, reminded me of God's promises when the path felt long, and encouraged me to finish what God placed within my heart. This book carries your fingerprints in more ways than words can express. I truly could not have done this without you.

To my beautiful daughter, **Beasley**, thank you for walking this journey alongside us with such grace, love, and encouragement. Your joy, support, and understanding have been a constant gift. You are deeply loved, and I am so thankful for you.

I would also like to express my sincere appreciation to **Katie Rios**, my wonderful editor. Thank you for your patience, encouragement, and the care you brought to every page. Your insight, discernment, and attention to detail helped bring clarity, flow, and life to these testimonies. You treated this book not just as a project, but as a calling, and your dedication has made a lasting impact. I am truly grateful for your excellent work and faithful partnership.

I also want to thank my dear friend, **Peter Steininger**, who has encouraged me to write this book for many years. You believed in what God placed within my heart long before it was ever written down. Your faith, friendship, and gentle persistence helped carry this vision forward, and I am deeply thankful for your support and encouragement through the years.

And above all, I give thanks to my Heavenly Father—the Lord Jesus Christ and the blessed Holy Spirit—for faithfully guiding me through this journey of more than 35 years of ministry. Every testimony, every encounter, and every word in these pages is a reflection of His mercy, grace, and faithfulness. Any fruit that comes from this book belongs to Him alone.

To God be all the glory.

Great things He has done.

With heartfelt gratitude,

ANTHONY

About the Author

Anthony and Annette Castro are the senior pastors of *Living Waters Christian Centre* in Tasmania, Australia. Together, they carry a shared passion to see lives transformed through the presence and power of God.

Anthony Castro is a revivalist with a deep burden to see the fire and glory of the Lord released in this generation. His ministry is marked by a passion to equip, train, impart, and release believers who burn with a love for Jesus and a hunger to see the gospel carried into a ripe global harvest.

Anthony oversees *Beulah Revival Network* in Campania, Tasmania, where he is helping to establish a revival training centre focused on raising up firebrand evangelists and leaders. Through teaching, impartation, and hands-on discipleship, he is committed to preparing men and women to be sent into the 10/40 Window and nations around the world.

With a strong emphasis on the ministry of the Holy Spirit, Anthony's heart is to encourage believers to move beyond information into intimate relationship—experiencing more of Jesus and releasing His life-giving power wherever they are sent. His ministry flows from a deep love for the presence of God and a desire to see ordinary people empowered to live Spirit-filled, Christ-centred lives for the glory of God.

APPENDIX

Chapter Discussion Questions

Discussion Questions Prepared in collaboration with the editorial team at Tall Pine Books.

CHAPTER 1: THE NIGHT HEAVEN INTERRUPTED MY PLANS

- Aunt Lupi's passionate invitation pulled young Anthony away from something he loved (the Dallas Cowboys playoffs) into an encounter that would shape his entire life. Can you recall a time when God interrupted your plans or comfort zone? What was your initial resistance, and how did that interruption ultimately redirect your path? How might you be more receptive to divine interruptions today?
- The chapter describes the atmosphere at the Kathryn Kuhlman service as moving from the thunderous "How

Great Thou Art" to the tender "He Touched Me." Why do you think this progression—from God's majesty to His nearness—was significant in preparing hearts for miracles? How does understanding both God's transcendence and His immanence shape our approach to worship and prayer?

- Anthony describes being "fully awake, caught up in the presence of God like never before" as a 12-year-old. What spiritual "hunger" or longing has been awakened in your own heart through encounters with God's presence? What practical steps can you take this week to cultivate that hunger and create space for God to move in fresh ways in your life?

Chapter 2: Where Hunger Became Encounter

- Anthony faithfully watched Kathryn Kuhlman's broadcasts every Sunday at 9 p.m. for two years, describing it as "a Sunday evening appointment with the Holy Spirit." What spiritual disciplines or "appointments" have you established with God? How has consistency in seeking Him—even through simple means like watching a program—deepened your relationship with the Holy Spirit?
- The chapter reveals how God orchestrated Anthony's airplane encounter with Captain John LeVrier's family, leading to a future meeting. Reflect on the concept of "divine appointments" versus coincidence. How do

we discern when God is sovereignly arranging connections in our lives? What role does our obedience play in recognizing and stewarding these moments?

- Anthony worked as a janitor, saving money without knowing it would fund his trip to Kansas City. God was preparing provision before Anthony even knew the need. Where might God already be preparing provision or resources in your life for something He's calling you toward? How does this truth about God's "advance preparation" change how you view your current circumstances or resources?

Chapter 3: Israel: A Call. A Confirmation. A Fire.

- When the Holy Spirit spoke to Anthony in Bethlehem saying, "Stay. Stay here and disciple My people," he immediately sought confirmation through prayer. Describe a time when you sensed God speaking to you about a major life direction. How did you seek confirmation? What helped you distinguish between God's voice and your own desires or fears?
- Anthony was given a paintbrush instead of a pulpit when he first arrived in Israel. The poster on his door reminded him: "Let us not grow weary while doing good, for in due season we shall reap if we do not lose heart" (Galatians 6:9). Why does God often prepare His servants through seasons of humble, hidden work before public ministry? How does this pattern reflect Jesus's own life and ministry?

- The LeTron retreat resulted in 30 young Palestinians being baptized in the Holy Spirit, speaking in tongues, and interceding powerfully. The chapter describes this as a "holy choir" and deep intercession with "groanings which cannot be uttered." Have you experienced or witnessed the Holy Spirit moving in such powerful, supernatural ways? What barriers (theological, cultural, or personal) might be hindering you from being open to the fullness of the Spirit's work in your life?

Chapter 4: The Miracle Worker in Bethlehem

- Anthony built his faith by repeatedly declaring, "Jesus Christ is a miracle worker in the city of Bethlehem"—even when he didn't initially feel it. The confession eventually became conviction. What declarations of faith do you need to speak consistently over your current situation, family, or calling? How might "faith coming by hearing" (Romans 10:17) apply to speaking God's promises aloud even before you see results?
- When Anthony prayed for Suha, he witnessed immediate, undeniable physical healing—water pouring from her body, swelling disappearing instantly. Yet modern Western Christianity often experiences healing differently or less dramatically. What factors might contribute to such powerful manifestations of healing in some contexts? How do we maintain faith for miracles while also honoring those who pray faithfully yet don't see instant results?

- Anthony concludes the chapter by inviting readers to declare: "Jesus Christ is the Miracle Worker in my life today." Take time right now to identify the specific area where you need Jesus to reveal Himself as the Miracle Worker. Write it down. Speak it aloud. Now commit to declaring this truth daily for the next 30 days, regardless of what you see or feel. What might change in your faith and circumstances through this practice?

Chapter 5: The Mountain Where Miracles Still Happen

- The chapter opens by describing the Mount of Olives as a place "where Heaven meets earth" and where "both pain and victory have left their mark." What physical places in your own journey hold spiritual significance—places where you've encountered God, experienced breakthrough, or walked through suffering? How do these locations shape your understanding of God's faithfulness?
- Anthony prayed for Samir in the hospital, then walked away and "forgot" about it, only to learn three months later of a complete healing. This raises profound questions about the nature of faith and healing. Must we always "feel" faith or see immediate results for God to work? How do we balance persistent, expectant prayer with the trust that releases outcomes fully to God's timing and sovereignty?

- When Anthony prayed, he declared: "Father, in the Name of Jesus, I ask You to give this man a testimony for Your glory." The focus was on God receiving glory through healing. How often do your prayers center on God's glory versus your comfort or desires? This week, reframe one major prayer request to specifically emphasize how God would be glorified through the answer—and notice how this shift affects your faith and perspective.

Chapter 6: Light Broke Through in Alexandria

- Anthony felt inadequate when the young blind girl asked for prayer: "I had prayed for many kinds of sickness before...but never for someone blind." Yet he prayed anyway, honoring her faith. Describe a time when you felt completely insufficient for what God was asking you to do. How did you respond? What did that experience teach you about God's power working through human weakness?
- The girl's healing unfolded gradually over three days—first light, then shadows, then full sight. This differs from the instant healings in previous chapters. Why might God heal in different ways and timeframes? What might progressive healing teach the recipient (and witnesses) that instant healing might not? How should this reality shape our prayers and expectations?

- Anthony notes that "to her, it was the miracle she had dared to believe for. To me, it was a reminder of the mercy and power of Jesus." The same event held different meanings for different people. Reflect on a "small" act of obedience you've offered to God—a prayer, an encouragement, a simple yes. How might that seemingly ordinary moment be extraordinarily significant in someone else's story? How does this truth motivate you to be faithful in "small" things?

Chapter 7: "Jesus Wore My Neck Brace"

- Rania's dream powerfully revealed that Jesus didn't just bear our sins on the cross, but also our sicknesses and pain. How has your understanding of the cross been primarily focused on forgiveness of sin? How does embracing the full reality of Isaiah 53:4-5—that "by His stripes we are healed"—change your view of what Jesus accomplished and what you can receive from Him today?
- Anthony prayed for Rania three times without visible results, then stepped back and "placed her gently into His hands, trusting, even though I did not understand." How do we navigate the tension between persistent prayer (Luke 18:1-8) and surrendered trust? When should we continue pressing in, and when should we release outcomes to God? What does this reveal about the nature of faith?

- The chapter ends with a prayer asking God to reveal "what 'neck brace' are you still wearing?" Pause and honestly ask the Holy Spirit: What pain, fear, wound, or burden have I been carrying that Jesus has already carried for me? Write it down. Now, in prayer, visualize Jesus on the cross wearing that burden—and practice releasing it fully to Him, choosing to walk in the freedom He purchased.

Chapter 8: From Dust to Snow to Fire

- Anthony's journey from Israel to Sweden to Cyprus came through unexpected invitations and prophetic confirmations, including his friend's vision of a red arrow on a map. How has God used unexpected sources—dreams, other people's words, unusual circumstances—to redirect your path? How do you discern whether these promptings are truly from God or merely good opportunities?
- The "Hidden School" in Cyprus trained young men who had left Islam to follow Christ, many at great personal cost and danger. These men couldn't return home and had to remain hidden for safety. How does this reality challenge Western Christianity's often comfortable, public faith? What does the existence of such costly discipleship in other parts of the world reveal about the true nature of following Christ?

- Farid's sister was healed in Jordan at the exact moment they prayed in Cyprus, demonstrating that "there is no distance in the Spirit." Think of someone you love who is geographically distant and facing difficulty (illness, spiritual struggle, hardship). Commit to interceding specifically for them this week, truly believing that the Holy Spirit can move powerfully across any distance. Record what you pray and watch for how God responds.

Chapter 9: A Voice That Cannot Be Silenced

- Nabil initially resisted the teaching on the baptism of the Holy Spirit, then encountered Jesus in a dream where Jesus said, "There's more if you want it." Have you ever resisted an aspect of God's work or Spirit because of theological discomfort, unfamiliarity, or fear? What would it mean for you to pray, "Lord, I want more of You—whatever that looks like"?
- The chapter describes Nabil's transformation from skeptic to Spirit-filled believer to television preacher reaching millions across the Arab world—all beginning with one midnight encounter. How do "hidden" moments of encounter with God often become the launching point for public ministry? Why does God seem to prioritize private transformation before public platform?

- Anthony writes that "the call of God rarely begins in comfort; it begins in surrender." Examine your own life: Where is God inviting you into uncomfortable obedience right now? What "yes" is He waiting for? What would happen if you stopped waiting to feel ready, adequate, or comfortable—and simply said yes to His invitation today, trusting Him with the outcome?

Chapter 10: The Yes That Changed Everything

- Anthony's journey to Russia came through a series of "yeses"—to Finland, to planting a church, to crossing borders, to preaching with expectation despite discouragement. Looking back on your own story, what "yeses" (even small ones) have proven to be turning points that led you toward God's greater purposes? How might God be inviting another "yes" from you today?
- The rehabilitation director told Anthony not to expect much fruit, yet 98% of the 150 former addicts responded to the gospel and many were healed. Anthony had to choose between agreeing with human limitation or believing God's promises. How do well-meaning people sometimes lower our expectations of what God can do? How do we honor others' experience while still maintaining bold faith for the impossible?
- The young woman who was healed of AIDS declared, "It's a miracle. Jesus healed me!" despite doctors saying it was impossible. Who in your life needs to hear

your testimony of what God has done? Are you boldly declaring His works, or have you allowed fear, doubt, or the opinions of others to silence your witness? This week, share one specific testimony of God's faithfulness with someone who needs hope.

Chapter 11: Resurrection Life, Way Down Under

- Anthony describes hearing "Australia" clearly in his spirit—a place he'd never considered. Sometimes God's direction comes as a complete surprise, unconnected to our plans or desires. Have you ever experienced God leading you somewhere or into something that seemed to come "out of nowhere"? How did you respond, and what did that journey teach you about God's perspective versus your own?
- After the man was declared dead for 67 minutes, Anthony prayed: "Give him another chance, Father—not only to be healed, but to know You." The prayer wasn't just for physical resurrection but spiritual salvation. How does this perspective transform how we pray for healing and miracles? What does it reveal about God's ultimate purposes in the supernatural—that they're always redemptive, not merely restorative?
- The book concludes by emphasizing that everything hinged on "a simple yes." God is not looking for perfection, expertise, or certainty—just willingness. As

you finish this book, what is the Holy Spirit highlighting to you? What is your "next yes"? Write it down as a commitment before God, and take one concrete step toward that obedience within the next 48 hours, trusting that your yes—however small it feels—can open heaven and change everything.

Index

E

F

G

H

I

J

K

L

M

S

T

U

V

W

Y

www.ingramcontent.com/pod-product-compliance
Lightning Source LLC
LaVergne TN
LVHW090944080826
845145LV00003B/883